THE NATURE of ORNAMENT

THE NATURE
of ORNAMENT

Rhythm and Metamorphosis
in Architecture

KENT BLOOMER

W. W. Norton & Company
New York • London

For information about permission to reproduce selections from this book, write to
Permissions, W. W. Norton & Company, Inc., 500 Fifth Avenue, New York, NY 10110

The text of this book is composed in ITC New Baskerville
with the display set in Folio
Manufacturing by Thomson-Shore, Inc.
Book design by Abigail Sturges

Library of Congress Cataloging-in-Publication Data

Bloomer, Kent C., 1935–
    The nature of ornament : rhythm and metamorphosis in architecture / Kent Bloomer.
        p. cm.
    Includes bibliographical references and index.
    ISBN 0-393-73036-0
        1. Decoration and ornament. 2. Decoration and ornament, Architectural. I. Title.

    NK1530 .B58 2000
    729—dc21   00-026935

W. W. Norton & Company, Inc., 500 Fifth Avenue, New York, NY 10110
W. W. Norton & Company Ltd., 10 Coptic Street, London WC1A 1PU

0 9 8 7 6 5 4 3 2 1

CONTENTS

ACKNOWLEDGMENTS

For nearly a quarter of a century the Yale School of Architecture has supported research and a course on architectural ornament. Without that support and the lively student participation in the course this book would not exist.

As the manuscript began to take shape, the Graham Foundation of Advanced Studies in the Fine Arts contributed generously to additional research and some of the costs of producing the final text and its images. The McDowell Colony provided the author with a tranquil residence during a crucial stage in the writing. An invitation to present ideas about ornament to the British Psychoanalytic Society reinforced some basic premises governing the psychological nature of ornament.

Outstanding architects with whom I have collaborated in the production of public ornament have enormously abetted my understanding of its grammar through direct practice. Charles Moore, Gerald Allen, Buzz Yudell, Brent Bowman, Cesar Pelli, and Peter Dominick stand out. Thomas Beeby deserves extraordinary thanks because, in addition to a large number of collaborations, he has provided strong scholarly arguments and fresh insights into the theory and history of ornament.

Philosophers have always untangled my thoughts. Karsten Harries relentlessly pointed to both the life and death of ornament's existence in modern times. Edward Casey marshaled thoughts that have helped me to locate ornament within the concept of "place." He has also acted as a critic capable of preventing digressions while opening avenues of inquiry into the subject.

THE NATURE OF ORNAMENT

Special thanks to Sharon Joyce, who examined difficult connections between visual ornament and visual language; to Suzanne Kelley, who edited the first comprehensive draft; to Jason Gaddis, who patiently and imaginatively compiled many of the final images; and to Nona Bloomer, for so much encouragement and help in writing this book.

The final shaping of the book was achieved by its editor, Nancy Green, and the philosopher–copy editor Kurt Wildermuth. I am extremely grateful to W. W. Norton for providing such able and thoughtful persons.

PREFACE

I study, teach, write about, and practice ornament because I believe its purpose—to articulate a realm of the imagination—is as important as it is misunderstood. Perhaps it is naive to hope that a deeper understanding of ornament will lead to a greater acceptance of its value. Yet that has been my own experience. The more I have unearthed the mystery of ornament, the more fascinating ornament has become, and the more I have become compelled to celebrate, even obsessed about celebrating, its life.

I have found it critical to set the essential nature of visual ornament apart from the increasingly specialized identities of other visual disciplines. Although it is an art form, ornament is neither "fine art" in the contemporary sense of the word nor what comes to mind when we speak of decoration. From this it follows that ornament is not simply a decorative art, although it participates in the activity of decorative artistry. Indeed, I believe that ornament is a category of art unto itself, a legacy with its own vocabulary and typology, and this view is supported by others who have chosen to investigate or practice ornament in depth, among them Owen Jones, Albert Racinet, Alois Reigl, Jessica Rawson, Joan Evans, and Henri Focillon. Ornament is not just another variation in the mainstream of visual expression, which itself has become rather limited to autonomous, self-contained, or complete works of art often meant to be understood or criticized apart from their settings.

In many respects, ornament needs a rigorous and perhaps even a narrow identity at this moment in its history. Neither a practice that is jaded nor a subject repressed by an overacademicized definition, ornament does not have to be liberated or expanded because it is barely standing on its own feet after a half-century of being avoided. An understanding of its cultural and psychological functions should be a subject of ongoing research, but such study would be best undertaken by restoring the core of ornament's timeless and perhaps original nature. The deepest nature of ornament is visible in its history and may be discerned with devoted examination and analysis. In the meantime, several principles might provide approaches to discovering ornament's nature:

- It is essentially driven by *line work* rather than mass, space, texture, color, materiality, or portraiture, though all these properties contribute to its visibility.
- Its organization is *rhythmic*; systems of geometry and proportion are subordinate.
- On the other hand, the *statics* of geometry and proportion are critical to the syntax between ornament and its objects.
- If we think of ornament as a *figuration* dependent upon multiple grounds, then one of its grounds must be the utilitarian form of its objects.
- However, ornament also represents things and actions that do not originate in utility; its meanings, therefore, are essentially *combinational*, and its figures tend to become *metamorphoses*.
- The life, the playfulness, and the fantasticality of ornament exist in the *liminal or transitional* space of its objects.

The importance of ornament in modern architecture may have become crippled by the profession's restricted use of the term *space*. For example, a colleague tells me he is not interested in ornament because it is not about space! How curious a misunderstanding. His comment may unconsciously reflect nineteenth-century theories of ornament, which focused upon the embellishment of construction in a time when the term *space* was hardly used at all in theories of architecture. But is it not construction and all its material and visual attributes that give architectural space its vivid existence? In Henri Focillon's words, "ornament art [was] perhaps the first alphabet of our human thought to come into close contact with space."[1] Here the term *space* is used in a profoundly psychological sense.

INTRODUCTION

This fear of ornament is part of the
protestantism of modern architecture;
it contains a sense of fending off some
insidious evil. Loos struck the appropriate
note in equating ornament with crime.

John Summerson[2]

The visual ornamentation of objects has been an article of culture for untold thousands of years. In the first century A.D., Vitruvius regarded ornament as an essential property of architecture. Leon Battista Alberti, writing in the fifteenth century and considered the father of the architectural profession, devoted four of his ten books on architecture to ornament, which he regarded as its noblest and most necessary attribute. In the following centuries, ornament flourished both in theory and practice; it became a historically based obsession in the nineteenth century. Yet for much of the twentieth century, especially during the second half, ornament has been cast in a pejorative light, and its study has been all but eliminated from the curricula of art and architecture schools.

For these reasons, an investigation into the nature, value, and potential of ornament, particularly public ornament, deserves serious attention. There appears to be a gradual renewal of interest in the subject in the public, professional, and academic realms, but such an investigation still requires overcoming negative prejudices and firming up the meaning of the term.

In this book, I attempt to identify the nature of ornament in a way that will assist designers and artists as well as art and architecture critics. I do not try to define ornament, because a "definition" would be too limiting for a term that alludes to an art form. Although I draw from the history of art and cultural theory, I presume to offer neither a history of art nor a cultural theory per se, but rather a brief summation, a synopsis, of some seminal moments and remarkable features of ornament that point to a theory of ornament. Indeed, one of the most intriguing properties of ornament is a certain consistency in the very basic kinds of meaning it provides throughout recorded history. Seemingly independent of differences in language and social and philosophical context, the term *ornament* possesses a distinctive etymology and its practice a timeless character that sets it apart from more changeful concepts such as *art* and *decoration* even as it participates in the activities innate to those disciplines.

At the same time, I attempt to analyze the intimate features of ornament, primarily the intricate rules of composition governing the emergence of visual figuration in it. I sidestep some important issues of local iconographies that have concerned many scholars of ornament and focus on the notion that ornament is a natural and universal system of human communication that can present a valuable segment of human thought. I argue that the phenomenon of ornament has virtues, indeed psychological functions, that are so specific as to be irreplaceable in the composition of culture. Although ornament can neither die nor become obsolete, there is historical evidence that its natural expression can be repressed.

But let us begin with a synopsis of meanings given to the term *ornament* over the centuries, keeping in mind the following question: Have the historical meanings of the term been sufficiently consistent to warrant the claim that ornament belongs to a distinct category of art, or does ornament refer to a practice that is subject to wide swings of interpretation?

THE NATURE of ORNAMENT

THE TERM *ORNAMENT*

Brief discussions about ornament are often tainted by contemporary uses of the term itself. *Ornament* comes loaded with conflicted and even negative meanings. Some associate ornament with excessiveness, frivolity, trivia, and superficiality, while others, perhaps especially those who enjoy ornament, relegate it to history as a repertoire of figures frozen in time. Many designers, especially architects, routinely avoid the term for fear that their professional function will not be taken seriously. In the presence of clients, they use euphemisms to disguise particular ornamental inclinations that might be associated with pretentious and uneconomic stuff.

Of course, prejudice has skewed the understanding of other fundamental terms as well. In the Victorian age, the word *sex* was fraught with all manner of unkind connotations, while in the early twentieth century, the word *feminine* carried implications of weakness and inferiority. Not to mention the long list of ethnic and national names employed as pejoratives! How curious that today the term *ornament*, which has been exalted for thousands of years, should find itself on the defensive.

The English word *ornament* comes from the Latin word *ornamentum*, rooted in *ornare*, which in a modern interpretation means "to confer grace upon some object of ceremony." The term *ornament*, by most accounts, originated inside the Greek term *Kosmos*, which meant something like "universe," "order," and "ornament." In such a Greek translation, ornament is implicated with concepts so vast that at first it may seem impossible to disentangle it from an inventory of all things.

1.1 The bud-and-blossom represents the everlasting cycle of organic regeneration. France, 19th century.

For the ancient Greeks, the word *Kosmos* was set in contrast to the word *Chaos*. Chaos preceded the emergence of the world as we know it, but was succeeded by Cosmos, which manifested the profound order of the world and the totality of its natural phenomena. In that respect, Cosmos made possible the knowable and thus the visible structure of the universe as the latter established the relations between its elements and its inhabitants. We might say that Cosmos could be represented as a consensus, a magnificent diagram, a universal tapestry, a comprehensive text, or, in the light of architecture, a supreme temple. Cosmic articles expelled chaos and revealed order.

In pre-Socratic culture, the totality of the universe was generally thought to be constituted by the Earth, the Heavens, and Eros. Eros is the god of love, and in antiquity the origin of the world was expressed in an act of procreation. Love was a uniting power that, treated either as a divinity or an idea, was responsible for the organization of the whole Cosmos and the achievement of union out of Chaos. In the beginning, Eros appeared and transformed the decomposed, dark, and stormy chasm of Chaos into the creation of the world. Elements formerly scattered were united into a productive embrace, and thus the earth and the skies, the wet and the dry, the cold and the hot were nurtured into specific locations, ranks, and degrees of animation. Eros was also described as intransigent, unconquerable, wandering, and among the dwellers of the wilderness capable of inciting madness and converting justice to evil. But those attributes did not prevent Eros from performing as an organizing force capable of controlling strife and conflict. Thus the forces of love and strife came to be understood as everlasting cycles that, like life, death, and the seasons, were to be manifested by visual figures (figure 1.1) that evoked rhythm and temporality. This vibrant world picture of order gained from desire, union, and rhythm was implicated with the earliest concepts of ornament, just as today rhythm is still poetically associated with feelings of unity.

In the ancient sense, Eros was an external agent, someone or something that could intervene to control the potentially chaotic entities of earth and sky. Eros intervened from without to convene worldly things like water, earth, fire, and air. As a metaphor, Eros seems analogous to what today we poetically identify as "nature," although the ancients treated such a nature as a more external or advening force than, for example, an internal human nature or an all-pervasive physics or chemistry.

If we return to the ancient Greek translation of *Kosmos* as "universe," "order," and "ornament," we can now begin to separate out ornament from the other two by imagining it to be like a force that unites

1.2 Ornament tends to be located in the periphery, between different kinds of things. U.S., 20th century.

and transforms conflicting worldly elements. Indeed, ornament seems to be a form of visual figuration that discloses cycles and tends to be located in the margin (figure 1.2) between different kinds of things.

The ancient Greek *Kosmeo* means "to arrange," "to order," and "to adorn," and "a woman Kosmése [adorns] herself in order to make her Kosmos visible."[3] Cities and societies adorn themselves as well. Specific

1.3 The ornamentation of the Temple of Zeus at Olympia (5th century B.C.) prepared it to honor the god.

Greek ornaments, those things impressed into cities, buildings, persons, and ceremonies, also mean that "something or someone . . . has been equipped or prepared, like a hunter, soldier, or priest. An ornamented temple (figure 1.3) is one prepared to honor the god."[4]

Vitruvius, in his *Ten Books on Architecture*, written in the Augustan first century, associated the word *ornament* with the figurative equipment, the representational things and their proportions, distributed upon elements of the Greek temples, such as the triglyphs and metopes, which embellished the orders, and the Ionic capital (figure 1.4), which "ornamented its front with cymatia [curved and wavy moldings] and with festoons of fruit arranged in place of hair."[5] He observed that "they [Greeks] brought the flutes down the whole shaft, falling like the folds in the robes worn by matrons." In these observations Vitruvius seems to focus on the articles and configurations—today we use a related term, *cosmetics*—that beautify and make visible that which ancient Greeks regarded as the forces of virtue. Vitruvius's choice of examples carries forward the ancient anthropomorphic metaphor with hints of Eros. Indeed, when he discusses the Corinthian order (figure 1.5) that was the most lavishly ornamented, he speaks of its imitating the slenderness of a youthful and attractive maiden. Feminine beauty, in the modern sense, was becoming implicated with *ornamentum*.

The medieval concepts of ornament resurrected some of the considerations of the ancient Greeks but with a focus more on the musings

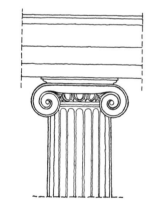

1.4 A typical Ionic capital.

of Pythagorus and Plato than on the gross anthropomorphism of the pre-Socratics. The Pythagoreans concentrated on the rational, particularly the role of numbers on the manifestation of natural energy and order, while Plato idealized and abstracted love in a direction that became less corporeal, more ideal, mental, and immaterial. Higher studies in the monastic schools were classified in the quadrivium of arithmetic, geometry, music, and astronomy. The product of those studies was displayed in the architecture of the cathedral as the temple of God. Each of these disciplines savored an amount of rational abstraction and divorce from the sensual. For the theologians of Chartres, "it was plausible to view matter as the building material, the creation proper as the 'adorning' of matter by the artful imposition of an architectural order."[6] Capable of manifesting astronomical music in its proportions, numbers, and geometry, the interior of the medieval cathedral was to become a spectacle of rational order in which ideal constellations were regularly distributed throughout the nave. Considered in the light of the ancient term *Kosmos* and its trilogy of universe, order, and ornament, the early medieval theorizing seems more disposed toward *order* than toward ornament. In chapter 8, "Gothic Metamorphosis," however, I argue that the subsequent emergence of Gothic tracery (figure 1.6), perhaps nudged by the rediscovered and more earthly thoughts of Aristotle, achieved the magnificent and sensual manifestation of Gothic ornament capable of embellishing the rigid organization of the basic architectural order. Were we to illustrate the term *ornament* in Gothic architecture, we would point to the tracery rather than the more fundamental elements of architectural order. Indeed, tracery, with its curvaceous and rhythmized line work, is a vibrant descendant of the cymatia, metopes, and foliations of Greco-Roman architecture, although it developed into an entirely novel species of visual figuration.

Alberti's treatise on the art of building, *De re aedificatoria* (1450), was the first translation of Vitruvius in the Renaissance. It was written at a moment when the provincial Gothic was being challenged by the urbane Italians. Books six, seven, eight, and nine discuss ornament and the ornamenting of sacred, public, and private buildings. For Alberti, the term *beauty* indicated a reflection of the wondrous works of nature. Beneath beauty in architecture there was mere utility, which he regarded as something we only recognize, whereas beauty is inherent to the architect's ordering of utility. In addition to those fundamentals, Alberti saw ornament as a form of heavenly light and complement to beauty. He thought that ornament, rather than being inherent, had

1.5 A Corinthian capital, the most lavishly ornamented order.

1.6 Gothic tracery on the exterior of the apse, Tabernacle Canopy, House of Jacques Koeur, Borges.

the character of something attached or additional to the utilitarian and inherent beauty of architecture. However, this act of attachment did not set ornament *apart* from architecture per se. Rather, ornament served to make the basically beautiful architectural order more visible. For Alberti, beauty was "the overall intellectual and primary frame-work—the essential idea—while ornament is the phenomenon—the individual expression and embellishment of this frame."[7] This triadic scheme identifies utility, beauty, and ornament as distinguishable and ascending properties within the project of architecture.

Alberti's discussion of ornament incorporated the entire cladding, the articulated outer skin of classical construction, as well as proportioned figural openings, such as important niches. Above all, he declared, "In the whole art of building the column is the principal ornament without any doubt; it may be set in combination, to adorn a portico, wall, or other form of opening, nor is it unbecoming when standing alone. It may embellish crossroads, theaters, squares."[8]

We must take into account here that fifteenth-century Italian architecture was a type of decorated wall construction in which the columns were both an optional and an often unnecessary means of structural support (figure 1.7). Thus Alberti's column was an added bearer of the virtue that originated in ancient architecture. The classical order containing the column elevated the building to the status of architecture by making visible the spirit of the lost Golden City of Rome as well as Alberti's venerable ancestry. The architectural elements being impressed upon the ordinary construction of the Renaissance were coming from a distant and sacred past.

Absent in Alberti's text, however, was a clear reference to the efficacy of cycles and of Eros incorporated in the ancient metaphor of *Kosmos*, although he clearly accepted as natural components the rhythmic figures of ornament belonging to the ancient Golden orders. Alberti allowed the auxiliary light of irrational ornament to flourish and become vividly manifest in the ordered beauty of his architecture, but his rational theory was not suited to the exploration of the specific meanings evoked by the cymatia and scrollwork. As John Summerson noted, though, there was an ambivalence in Renaissance thought between the rational and the romantic. Alberti presented the rational side of architecture in the same period in which the poet Francesco Colonna imagined architecture as a place of love and procreation. Colonna's poem "The Dream-Love-Strife of Poliphilus" depicts a lover searching for a perfect union with his mistress. In a moment of passion, Poliphibus flees into an enchanted forest, in which he encounters an ancient palace, and there he is united with his mistress. Evidently, for

1.7 Alberti's columns were often adherent elements that bore the virtues of a classical architectural tradition.

1.8 Rococo ornament on the pulpit of the Die Wies Pilgrimage Church. 18th century.

Colonna, the ancient architecture was not just an orderly work of exquisite geometry; it was also a place in which the power of Eros held court. For Colonna, the temple was a place of mediation as well.

Certainly, the most theatrical productions descended from the Renaissance occurred in the late baroque and rococo architecture (figure 1.8) that culminated in the mid-eighteenth century. Figures of ornament became increasingly more daemonic and rhythmically frenetic, as though they were struggling with an excessively prescribed orderliness in the basic architectural form. Yet in the baroque period the walls become curvaceous and the architectural settings more spectacular. It was a period of music and architecture in which the word *embellishment* became almost synonymous with the term *ornament*. Embellishment (from the French *en + bel*) is a means of bringing beauty into something from without, although in baroque and rococo architecture such embellishment was not thought to be apart from the basic architectural scheme. Indeed, embellishment was becoming implicated more with elements of *space* than with elements of construction.

The rococo ornament of the eighteenth century extolled the power of Eros to mediate between the domains of heaven and Earth. Building upon the theatricality of the baroque, the architecture of Bavarian churches and palaces became particularly pictorial as it employed and positioned representational painting and sculpture in the space of buildings. Explicit paintings of scenes from an ecstatic ascent to heaven filled the ceilings, while the lowest arcades of construction were prosaic and earthly. High up in the naves of churches, there often was a turbulent band of rocaille figuration that evoked "rock and conch, coral and reed, water, wave and foam . . . the pattern of surging and plunging."[9] "This mediating function [of rocaille] can itself be taken as a figure of the Virgin . . . the miraculous site of the wedding of sky and water."[10] Here the great bands of ornament are distributed within a transitional zone, a cartouche binding the sacrament between the deity and Earth, in which the heavens are not depicted by ornament per se but rather by frescoes creating pictorial illusions of a virtual world above and beyond the ornament. The rococo cartouche is positioned as a rhythmic figuration between two realms.

In the eighteenth century, one could point to the rocaille and say "that is ornament," and thus the terms *ornament, embellishment*, and *rococo* almost converged. Rocaille could be perceived in whole cloth and therefore understood as a fantastic but knowable type of figuration like tracery, although unlike tracery it did not as clearly issue from the earthly shafts of construction building upward from the ground. Rocaille was more of an airborne entity, a dream figure, and as such more suited to separation from the rigorous taxonomy of basic structural elements.

In the nineteenth century, the term *ornament* came more and more to mean something applied to architecture, although its value and fascination were not diminished. To the contrary, the century was a riot of ornament (figure 1.9) and was in some ways one of its most marvelous and inventive periods. However, a theoretical understanding of the

*1.9 Victorian ornament
in the interior of All Saints,
London, 19th century.*

linkages between ornament and architecture was confused by several
major developments, foremost among them being the Enlightenment
and the triumph of the rational over the irrational. Consider that,
although the forces of Eros were powerful in their ability to bond dis-
parate elements and to suppress conflict, they were nevertheless sublime, unpredictable, and notably wanting in nineteenth-century scien-

tific justification. Concurrently, many customary understandings and acceptances of ornament were called into question by an increasing academic and professional recognition of the historic validity of many architectural styles resulting from multiple national origins. The conventional and venerable ornament descended directly from the Greco–Roman model was challenged, and thus the very nature of exemplary ornament was subject to debate. Surprising examples of ornament appeared for the first time in works being imported, for example, from Egyptian, Japanese, and American Indian culture. The ability to illustrate the meaning of the term by precedents was becoming more of an anthropological and art-historical responsibility. From the popular standpoint, the acceptance of different types of ornament was becoming a matter of taste and fashion. How could there be a general understanding of the mediating or reconciling function of specific visual figurations that alluded to an unfamiliar cosmos?

Coincident with the internationalization of architecture history, the appearance of new technologies, new materials of construction, and unprecedented types of buildings such as the railroad station and the art museum disrupted conventions governing the appropriate distribution or location of ornament upon particular works, elements, and types of building. One consequence was a tendency to treat ornament as an appliqué taken out of a pattern book of one style or another and thus to define ornament as a commodity to be aesthetically or decoratively attached rather than as a profound property of architecture and design. In order to prevent the noticeably added and seemingly superficial application of ornamental figures, many architects chose mature historical styles in which the sensitive relationship or the syntax between ornament and the greater body of architecture was sufficiently established to allow gradual and novel modification of detail. By remaining the property of an established style, the term *ornament* could be folded into the history and letters of that style, and thus the distribution of ornament would be expected to follow the customary rules and grammar of a particular tradition. This practice often required the term *ornament* to be qualified as *Greek ornament, Gothic ornament, rococo ornament*, etc., with all the attendant implications and meanings. Such an eclectic approach made the definition of the term *ornament*, standing alone, rather abstract.

Another approach, perhaps the most difficult, was to formulate universal principles of ornament and to treat it as a phenomenon that could be understood transculturally and transchronologically. The term *ornament*, although it relied largely on an understanding of

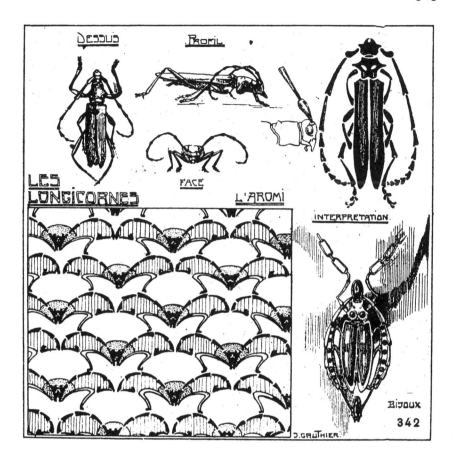

1.10 Rules and systems were formulated for the production of ornament. France, 20th century.

precedent, would be described somewhat philosophically or psychologically as a particular property of human thought and expression. To some extent, its rules and functions could be formulated and its limits prescribed (figure 1.10). In this respect, ornament would be a category of design and architecture with its own peculiar history and future. Augustus Pugin, John Ruskin, Christopher Dresser, Gottfried Semper, Louis H. Sullivan, and Alois Reigl followed this approach. They sought to define ornament by postulating principles of design. For instance, in his book *The Art of Decorative Design* (1862), the Victorian designer and author Christopher Dresser called ornament that which "super-added to utility renders the object more acceptable through bestowing upon it an amount of beauty which it would not otherwise possess."[11] The first level of addition in Dresser's scheme refers to a preliminary fleshing out of raw utilitarian elements into well-proportioned and conventionalized architectural forms. He went on to say how that might be done and provided detailed examples. Perhaps influenced by Ruskin's

Seven Lamps of Architecture (1849), he later expanded the term *beauty* to include a list of attributes such as fitness, order, humor, power, and passion. Although Dresser was more a Gothic revivalist than a Greco-Roman classicist, there is an interesting correspondence between his concept of superadding to an improved level of utility and Alberti's notion of ornament as an auxiliary light added to the previously added frame of beauty. In both theories, a kind of basic order is first demanded of the otherwise chaotic bedrock of utility in order to further admit ornament. In both, there are triads in which ornament is treated as the final fulfillment of a work of architecture that, because of its original connection to the bedrock of utility, is able to hold on to full membership in the architectural scheme.

By the end of the century, the term *ornament* began to acquire an academic definition or identity, which attempted to summarize the various universal considerations that had accumulated over the centuries. A Cantabrigian account in 1911 declared ornament to be an

> element which adds an embellishment of beauty in detail. Ornament is in its nature accessory, and implies a thing to be ornamented, which is its active cause . . . [although] it does not exist apart from its application. Nor is it properly *added* to a thing already in existence, . . . but is rather such modification of the thing *in the making* as may be determined by the consideration of beauty.[12]

Again the implication is that beauty belongs to an element that is accessory to "the merely utilitarian plan from the point of view of art,"[13] yet an accessory that is necessary to fulfill the primary architectural intent.

This brief summary of the historical treatment of the term *ornament* reveals shifts in meaning as vast as the development and vicissitudes of Western culture. Those shifts of meaning are often cited by scholars as resulting from the mysterious and the extremely specific contexts that, for being in the past, may be of little value to modern culture. On the other hand, taken in relation to the design of objects, the ancient Greek, medieval, Renaissance, and turn-of-the-century scholars are saying more or less the same thing, which is that ornament incorporates an amount of adherence into something that possesses and manifests an inherent utilitarian form. That adherence may range from reflections on the fixed order of the heavens to the manifestations of cycles, procreative forces, and elements of beauty in nature.

The identity of the term *ornament*, therefore, has always depended on the incorporation of other considerations into the fabric of practical objects—considerations that might fulfill a picture of the world in which the object is performing. That accomplishment is essentially combinational, which is to say that ornament functions as a visual system or type of configuration capable of apprehending and uniting multiple meanings. Such an act of combining may not have to be as culturally specific as it must be visually intelligible.

The principal strategy required to achieve an image of combination in ornament is to present a spectacle of transformation. In that spectacle, it may appear that one thing is turning into another and vice versa. When Henri Focillon, in *The Life of Forms in Art*, exquisitely identifies ornament as "the chosen home of metamorphoses," he makes ornament into a habitat that allows metamorphosis.

Within that habitat, the primary facts and expressions of utility, which are present and potentially visible in the construction and space of any practical object, are in the first order of things to be transformed.

2.1 Ancient Panamanian pedestal
bowl that also served as a functional
container. 7th–9th century.

UTILITY

Every meaning requires a support, or
a vehicle, or a holder. These are the bearers
of meaning, and without them no meaning
would cross from me to you, or from you
to me, or indeed from any part of nature
to any other part.

George Kubler[14]

The dependence upon expressions of utility for an amount of its meaning immediately distinguishes ornament from those projects of today's fine art in which the art object is an aesthetically self-sufficient entity. Utility indicates the economic, the practical, and the necessary, realms we also associate with work. "Fine" expressions of art, as opposed to crafts or the industrial arts, seek independence from utility as they isolate desires and figments of the imagination. Recently, for example, preferring to be seen as fine artists rather than artisans, to have their work identified as pure art rather than mere craft or industrial articles intended to perform a specific task, some potters have gone so far as to prevent their clay vessels from holding water.

From the beginning, however, Western ornament has rarely sought to disrupt or overwhelm utility but rather has aimed to function as a parergon, which is an accessory to work. It is distributed upon objects to provide a vision or world picture that is absent in the mere expression of utility. Indeed, Greco-Roman, Gothic, and Victorian ornament benefited dramatically from the forceful and supportive presence of utility as it simultaneously moved to express things beyond utility.

Apprehending some of the significance of ornament means consciously or unconsciously taking in the meanings of the work its objects were made to perform. For example, the pedestal bowl from ancient Panama (figure 2.1) is first of all a simple functional container often associated with liquids. The ancient potter took care to produce an elegant, useful, and familiar vessel. Within the bowl, serpen-

2.2 The line detailing on a Rhodian amphora engages the functional shape of the vessel.

tine line work forms zoomorphic figures, which combine organically with the refined shape of the bowl. The ornament, like water, is fluid and contained. The distribution of its figuration is limited by the useful space. As the lines circulate over the surface, the taut energy within the central scroll at the bottom of the bowl moves to the outer rim or horizon. The lines seem "to merge with its background while, at the next moment, the background seems to come forward as an active part of the figure."[15] Anthropologist Mary H. Helms regards this particular exchange between figure and material ground as a "cosmovision" revealing a potent interaction between the extraordinary world and the ordinary bowl.

The line work embellishing a sixth-century Rhodian amphora from Kameiros (figure 2.2) engages the shape of a more complex yet practical vessel designed for storing wine. Although the amphora and the Panamanian bowl both have scrolls and rhythmic border motifs, they allude to different kinds of natural forces as metaphors of life. The ornament of the Greek vessel evokes the radiance of a plant upon an outer surface rather than the daemonism of an animal upon an inner surface. In the amphora, the line work conforms to the external form of the vessel. The spiral scrolls or tendrils occupy the curvaceous portions, while the linear swastikas occupy the more rigid and tapered cylindrical neck piece. To the extent that we may regard this as an evocation of Greek thought, we witness the life-forms of a world in which things are driving upward from the ground toward a more abstract and formal realm above, a dynamic directionality reinforced by the absence

2.3 A punch bowl illustrates duality between the ordinary and extraordinary. England, 19th century.

of figures around the bottom and the burgeoning of the palmette fans about the shoulder or ledge.

The nineteenth-century punch bowl (figure 2.3) illustrates yet another world picture. The designer, Gottfried Semper, who called for a "duality" between expressions of the ordinary and of the extraordinary, emphasizes the most fundamental and practical portions of the bowl by simply rendering them as naked. The moldings at the base and joints, the lower body of the bowl, and the outer surfaces of the lid and handles are plain and polished. Upon the remaining surfaces of the bottom and middle sections as well as the head piece, a carnival of fantastic people, waves, festoons, and efflorescing nature conveys a playful vision of humans occupying a festive world beyond the bowl. Sentinels sit and squat around the base as guardians of the punch, while revelers frolic around the body. Others emerge from the waves to support the handles.

2.4 A delicate capital erupts from a functional and rigid post. Wells Cathedral.

In the much more complex fabric of buildings, many visual dualities may exist at a variety of scales and sites. A leafed capital and scrolled brackets erupt from the crowns of supporting posts at the ground level (figures 2.4 and 2.5). The columns are plain, practical, erect, and clearly pushing upward to support the weight of the roof. The upward force is carried into the efflorescent figures of ornament, which by themselves, set apart from the posts and brackets, might become lifeless fragments.

A festooned picture frame hovers inside the space of a grand window overlooking the Hudson River north of New York City (figure 2.6). The small embellished window inside the enormous window acquires grandeur and power from the greater opening in which it is situated as well as the majestic view of the Hudson it contains. The rhythms and polychrome geometry running around the picture frame establish another place, a microcosm whose extraordinary existence is charged by its magnificent architectural frame.

2.5 A bracket becomes a foliated scroll. U.S., 19th century.

Louis Sullivan distributed his "Celtic" scrolls upon the surface of a large, typical, and practical hinge holding the doors of the Getty Tomb. The potential of rotation inherent in the hinge precedes and activates the capricious and spiraling antics of the ornament (figure 2.7), yet there is a visible interaction of actual and virtual energy.

Our lives are dependent upon practical and mundane objects. We cannot escape that reality over time. Moreover, we develop a very basic understanding of practical things as well as the space that services those things. We carry that knowledge inside us even when our imaginations are free to roam. Such knowledge, indeed such reality, can be har-

2.6 A window inside a window, Lyndhurst. Tarrytown, NY, 19th century.

nessed and put to work as fuel for the motions, apparitions, and surprises of ornament's figuration. The weights and thrusts of necessity can be tapped to shape festoons and to generate spirals.

Certain ideas can be best understood when they are presented in concert with the power and reality of a practical function. If I were to describe with words alone the meanings articulated by the Panamanian, Rhodian, and Victorian vessels, or the architectural post, bracket, window piece, and hinge, I would produce a cumbersome text devoid of the inherent energy, purpose, substance, and firm enclosure of a particular object or specific place. The extraordinary ideas in visual ornament combine with the material and spatial economies of useful objects in order to tap the powers inherent in the shapes of those objects. In this way, utility authorizes and fuels ornament, which, in turn, awakens mundane objects from the necessity of their everyday work. In the words of John Ruskin, "when the mind is informed beyond the possibility of mistake as to the true nature of things, the affecting it with a contrary impression, however distinct, is no dishonesty, but on the contrary, a legitimate appeal to the imagination."[16]

2.7 The functional motion of the hinge activates the potential energy within the spiral of the ornament. Louis Sullivan, Carrie Eliza Getty Tomb, Graceland Cemetery, Chicago, 1890.

3.1 Everyday utilitarian objects are the primary carriers of ornament.

THE LINGUISTIC NATURE OF ORNAMENT

The closest synonym employed in modern speech for the term *ornament* is *embellishment*, which means something that has come into the body of a practical object from without. The term *decoration*, on the other hand, implies a pleasing arrangement of things and a suggestion of the decorous, a condition marked by propriety, good taste, good conduct, and good appearance. To decorate is to arrange things in a manner that indicates high, proper, and pleasing standards, while ornament connotes only the presence of meaningful and seemingly adherent elements pervading an arrangement. A decorative element may be an ornament if it brings something from outside the object, but a pure decoration may simply be an artifact or pleasant thing placed on a table or a wall. It is possible to say that a tasteful distribution of ornament is decorative, but we cannot so easily say that a horrific distribution of ornament is decorative. In all cases, the rigorous distribution of ornament may be called ornamentation.

Ornament can be offensive as well as gracious. Ornament's intrusive property was observed by those who in the late nineteenth and early twentieth centuries condemned it for being impure or excessive. They assigned those attributes to nonacceptable articles, ones lacking good taste and good manners. It is telling that while the practice of the decorator, especially the interior decorator, ascended in the last 150 years, no equivalent profession of "ornamenter" came into being. In colloquial usage, the term *ornament* has remained more disturbing or more daemonic than the more neutral term *decoration*.

To call ornament impure by virtue of its bringing some adherent things to an object or place suggests that it participates in a process of informing. In this respect, we may characterize ornament as a type of language in which visual thoughts, worldly ideas, communal ethos, and memories may be directly deposited and communicated within the substance of material objects and places. Those who would prefer to limit the term *linguistics* to the study of spoken language, that is, lingua as tongue, might treat ornament as a semblance of spoken language that displays some of its features. Either way, it is not difficult to demonstrate the existence of visual and spatial systems of communication with their own forms of grammar and capacities for narration. Certainly, we can imagine a repertoire of body gestures as communicative or a deliberate spatial arrangement of signs, pictures, and shapes as belonging to a process in which ideas are exchanged and developed as active agents in the rhetoric of a culture.

The basic elements of speech itself may originally have been derived from spatial figures. Anthropologist Mary Foster has suggested that certain characteristic sounds evolved from the configuration of oral gestures, such as the position of the lips, tongue, and teeth and contractions of the larynx, and that those primordial visual and spatial gestures produced an ancient repertoire of analogic references that functioned as the units of a primitive vocabulary.[17] The meanings originally associated with those gestural sounds may not have survived as codes consciously embedded in the meanings of modern speech. However, Foster's recognition that spatial gestures can function as the vocabulary of a nonphonetic system of communication, thus endowing two- and three-dimensional forms with a seminal status in the development of human thought, is valuable to the consideration of ornament as languagelike.

Samuel Taylor Coleridge speculated that the "primary art" of visual gesture as codified in writing acts as a mediation between humanity and nature. He saw a progression in the history of writing in which "First there is gesticulation; then rosaries or wampum; then picture language; then hieroglyphics; and finally alphabetic letters."[18] In these visual codes Coleridge saw a "reconcilement between the external and the internal." His chronicle is of particular interest if we interpret "rosaries" as chanting and "wampum" as ornament and locate them between mere gesticulation and picture language.

Indeed, as I discuss further in chapter 6, "Rhythmized Foliation," elemental figures of ornament are extraordinarily gestural. Intricate line work within patterns of ornament appears to wave and swing, sometimes radiating outward in exclamation and other times swirling inward and pointing to meaningful symbols deposited in the interior of its composition. If, moreover, we abstract the gesturing hands and gesturing bodies of everyday communication into geometric shapes, the shapes correspond neatly to many of the fundamental markings universally found in ornament, such as spirals and zigzags.

Coleridge's notion of rosaries as a development beyond basic gesture may be read as a reference to plotting a sequence of gestures for emphasis and to develop a narrative over time. His "rosaries" are comparable to a form of chanting in which an idea is emphatically reiterated and reaffirmed, a rhetorical device that survives in modern poetry and oratory. It is striking to observe that in the history of ornament there is an abundance of figural repetition, almost to the point that repetition seems thematic to the very essence of ornament in the same way that repetition is regarded as a hallmark of poetry. In addition, despite their primitive status, gesture, repetition, and rhythm remain basic properties of modern speech and have not been jettisoned from our ordinary lives by advances in the rigidity of alphabetic, denotative, and scientific writing.

Within the language of ornament is a vocabulary consisting of a repertoire of both meaningful and provocative gestures and figures (figure 3.2). The grammar of this visual language stems from the interactive arrangement between distinct figures as well as the special ways in which their patterns, or passages, are distributed upon the terrain of objects. Within those passages, gesture seems to be employed as an interrelational or grammatical device in addition to functioning as an element of vocabulary like a word. The means of transmitting the rhythmic passages exists in the agency and the presence of the object of ornamentation (figure 3.1), be it a utensil, a hat, a building, or a letterform. In *The Book of Kells*, for example, written in the ninth century in a moment of intense brilliance with respect to the ornamenting of letters, "the strong tendency of the different [ornaments] to combine together, forming in some cases a continuous, ever-shifting pattern, is also the mark of a time when all the motifs have been accepted and absorbed to a point where they come together like the letters of a word or the words of a sentence (figure 3.3)."[19] The Celtic example also illustrates that ornaments cannot be separated from a particular place or object lest they become merely autonomous figures, symbols, artifacts, or objets d'art.

Yet it is precisely in the need to make material contact with an object that a similarity between the language of ornament and the lan-

3.2 The curvilinear forms of the black moresques are provocative gestures. Rudolph Wyssenbach folio. Germany, 16th century.

3.3 The separate ornamental motifs harmonize on the page to become like words in a sentence. Matthew I, I: Liber generationis, Book of Kells. Ireland, 8th–9th century.

guage of words ends and a crucial distinction begins. Alphabetic writing and speech are portable systems of communication and do not have to materially bond with other things in order to function. Because ornament depends on the particularities of the object or place being ornamented, it cannot evolve into a mobile and self-contained medium. In contrast, modern written language depends neither on the shape of its letters nor upon the materiality of their immediate location for its essential meaning. *Speech* is entirely liberated from the material constraints of location. The necessity for a rigorous bond between an ornament and the place being ornamented implicates the meanings peculiar to ornament with the functional, material, and memorable properties of location.

Compare, for example, how words and ornaments are conventionally located on a page; the former occupy a tier of parallel slots, whereas the latter often run around the margins (figure 3.4). Systems of ornament seek the edges, openings, and voids of the places in which they might constellate their repertoire of figures, whereas the conventional pattern underlying the organization of words is an array of channels equal in length and height that serve as ideal containers for the portable figures of speech. Letters are shaped by the channels into graphic units of common size. The shape of the page does not fundamentally affect the significance of words; its form is no more important than the empty space of a computer screen.

On the other hand, when we place figures of ornament on an object, their location is critical. Rather than distributing them in the invariable linear pattern of words in sentences, we usually arrange them at the outer edge of the object, or disperse them evenly in a repetitive pattern, such as a diaper pattern, or place them intensively within a zone at the center of the object. Ornaments bring their own spatial requirements and motility while simultaneously seeking responsive locations inherent to their objects. Thus the shape of each object participates directly in the grammar of ornament even as the object's own form is visually altered by the ornamental pattern.

Ornament at the edge of an object may suggest the physical boundary of a sacred domain (a world edge). In another allegory or cosmovision, the same object's center may be given the highest status. The object acts as a landscape to be occupied and subdivided into a variety of meaningful sites. Corners (figures 3.5 and 3.6) may become a definite place or a cusp capable of gathering and deflecting figures

3.4 Words are distributed in parallel slots, whereas ornament seeks margins and edges.

3.5, 3.6 Corners may become a definite place by either concentrating or deflecting ornament.

3.7 A homogenous distribution of ornament suggests an all-pervading authority of a particular institution. Jean de Blondel, The Bible of Jean de Vandetar. France, 14th century.

of ornament. In this respect, the homogeneous distribution of ornament upon the entirety of a surface may indicate the all-pervading authority of a particular institution (figure 3.7).

But if ornament is the meaningful form of communicative chanting proposed by Coleridge, how does its storytelling become a profound property of static and rigidly material objects? How does the viewer avoid perceiving the narrative figures of ornament as labels like written messages simply stuck onto the unique surfaces of an object rather than being a grammatical property of the entire object? We can answer this question if we grant that an object has a basic capacity to make a statement without the incorporation of ornament. In other words, a well-formed practical object clearly states a purpose and a potential for a variety of uses by virtue of its basic shape. That shape inevitably promotes and informs whatever meanings and metaphors we can further attach to its unique function. The storytelling capacity of ornament, therefore, takes an object's unique function, that is, its primary statement, into account and employs it as a fundamental theme in the unfolding of a narrative capable of revealing other functions and other themes. Indeed, ornament is a language dependent on the combination of at least three levels of meaning, one of which is inherent to its object without ornament. The integration of ornament to its object is therefore achieved through the linguistic, or perhaps we should say grammatical, integration of those multiple levels into a single articulate composition. Those three levels, or sources of meaning, may be described as follows:

1. The most basic source of meaning found in ornament is the fact of its object's utility; for example, a bowl may mean something that contains something else, a window may mean something we look through to another place, and an arch may mean something we walk through to another place (figure 3.8). A post proclaims the act of supporting.

3.8 An external arch signifies an entrance or exit. Louis Sullivan, Auditorium, Chicago, 1887–89.

3.9 Victorian table settings reflect a contemporary interest in the forms of the natural world beyond their inherent utility. England, 19th century.

Such crude utilitarian facts may be elaborated into metaphors, so that the bowl comes to evoke the containing of all sorts of things, from coins to ten thousand spectators and even to the regional importance of a particular football game. A window might be regarded as a moment of discovery or escape. A post might allude to strength and stability. However, those factual meanings and metaphors are not necessarily equipped or prepared at the outset to combine grammatically with meanings that have originated elsewhere.

2. Adherent meanings, provided by the *world at large*, may theoretically be taken from an inventory of all things and all actions beyond those originating in a particular utility. Fortunately, such an expansive inventory is always restrained by a culture's particular dreams, desires, or visions, or perhaps we might say its special interests in the world at large as well as its sense of what is lacking in the expressions limited to those originating in the object's utility. For example, if a particular culture believed that all things could be expressed with bowls or the bowls' extended meaning of containment, then nothing would be deemed lacking and the bowl need only be refined or elaborated to heighten its importance. To decorate the bowl would be merely aesthetic. But humans have always demonstrated an inclination to exceed the limits of utility. The Victorians, who were showered with machine-made objects, longed for the vitality, repose, and beauty of trees and flowers (figures 3.9). They wanted their objects and buildings to recall the nourishing cycles and products of botanical nature seemingly suppressed in the midst of the grime and the labor of industrialization. The same world that produced Darwin and the steam locomotive was fascinated by the patterns originating in crystals, snowflakes, and the

3.10 The portrait of the head, per se, is not necessarily ornament, but it is framed by ornament.

3.11 A portrait in the Book of Kells.

living forms of terrestrial nature, although specific representations of nature by themselves are seldom prepared to function as ornament. If we simply represent a certain object or portray a particular person and place the portrait upon a wall (figures 3.10 and 3.11), we have not necessarily produced ornament (although we may frame such objects with

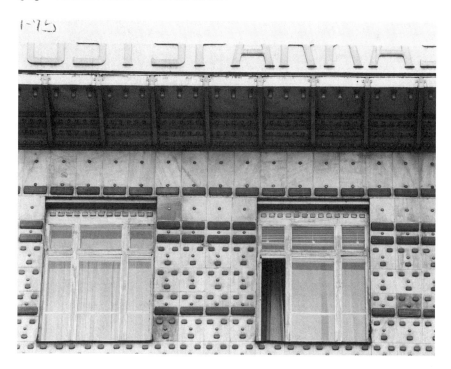

3.12 Simply elaborated structural elements are not necessarily ornament. Facade, Post Office, Vienna, 20th century.

3.13 Inherent and adherent forces and elements combine within ornament.

ornament). Similarly, if we merely elaborate upon structural elements in the design of building (figure 3.12), we have not necessarily produced ornament. If the literal meanings of the portraits and structural elements can exist intact while apart from the wall and appear as though they could be readily placed somewhere else, they would be an independent elements of decoration, pieces of autonomous art, or merely elegant details of construction.

3. The visual achievement of combining and uniting the expressions of utility and the expressions of adherent things from the world at large is an act of mediation that occurs *within* the limited and transitional space of ornament (figure 3.13). Within that space, the literal meanings found in the inherent and adherent contexts are further abstracted, fragmented and recombined rhythmically[20] into the fantastic vocabulary of a completely unique system of communication capable of developing or revealing dreams, potentials, memories, and resolutions, and even of telling stories, albeit sometimes nonsensical and fantastical. As I discuss further in chapter 5, "Rhythm," and chapter 6, "Rhythmized Foliation," syntactic mechanisms within ornament's configuration (figure 3.14) are capable of admitting, heightening, involuting, and driving together the contextual fragments in meaningful inventions constituting a form of narrative while proceeding to give

"birth to an entire flora and fauna of hybrids that are subject to the laws of a world distinctly not our own"[21] (figure 3.15).

However, before any of the meaningful shapes or figures that originated outside the space of ornament can be incorporated into the language of ornament, their original and autonomous identities must be prepared, modified, and specially equipped with a graphic or sculptural capacity to combine with each other as well as with the object. Such preparatory modification results from a process of *conventionalization*, or we might say architecturalization, of literal things, shapes, and forms.

3.14 Curving sculptural lines drive together the fragments, such as the heads, into a powerful composition. Mexico, 18th century.

3.15 Ornament gives birth to hybrids that seem to belong to another world. U.S., 19th century.

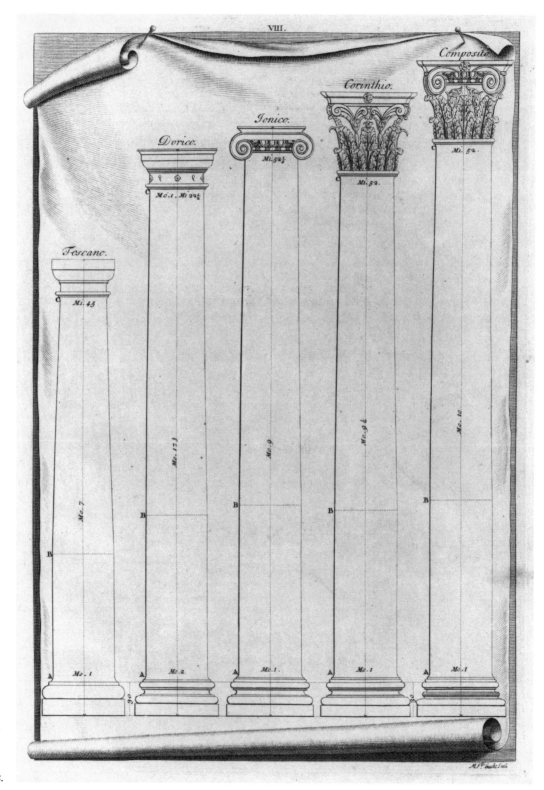

4.1 Theorists have prescribed specific proportions for the five classical orders.

CONVENTIONALIZATION

In nineteenth- and early twentieth-century theories of ornament, the term *conventionalized* indicates a social consensus in which a figure has acquired a shared identity, an acceptance, and thus an intelligibility. In this way, the conventionalized ornament is like a conventional word. It further indicates that a natural figure has been abstracted from its native shape in order to convene with the materiality, form, and inherent expressions of an object.

Prior to the nineteenth century, a conventionalized figure of architectural ornament was thought to have always been there, so to say, by belonging to the original and classical forms of building. A repertoire of basic motifs had been reiterated over the centuries to become customary, sanctioned, and perfected. In Western architecture, "the acanthus leaf (figure 4.2) and the whole world of floral motives in both classical and medieval art belong in this category,"[22] as well as the egg-and-dart-molding, the Ionic volute, and the Greek key. The broad recognition and acceptance of conventionalized classical ornament in the Western world matched the long-standing belief in the authority of classical architecture as seminal, singularly generic, and the origin of all architecture worthy of the name. Indeed, theorists have labored from the Renaissance to the present to prescribe the correct shapes, proportions, and locations of such conventionalized ornaments and their subordination to the ancient Doric, Ionic, Corinthian, Tuscan, and composite orders of architecture (figure 4.1). The very concept of architecture was virtually indistinguishable from the Greco-Roman

4.2 The acanthus leaf, a basic motif, has been repeated so often as to become customary, sanctioned, and perfected.

4.3 Ornament, once
refined in stone, has been
appropriated for the cast-iron
shafts running up the front
of a nineteenth-century
office building.

model as well as the ancient model's influence on medieval architecture. Proven by history, the venerable ornaments were the truly conventionalized ones, a state of affairs that, in effect, defined ornament per se as a conventional phenomenon.

However, early in the nineteenth century, conventionalization became a thorny problem. On the one hand, Greco-Roman and medieval classicality was no longer regarded as the exclusive origin of architecture, as the ancient buildings of Northern Europe, Asia, Egypt, and Native America were studied in the art and architecture academies. Imperialism and world travel alerted Westerners to the multiple origins of world culture. By mid-century, national "styles" proliferated, and entirely novel examples of ornament from Asia were being exhibited in Western museums. During the same period, new types of buildings, such as the public museum and the railroad station, began to displace the palace and the church as public monuments. New methods and materials of industrialized construction upset the traditional ways of fabricating ornament and physically integrating it into the elements and details of building. How could an acanthus leaf refined in the ancient orders, for example, be appropriate on mass-produced, cast-iron shafts running up the multistoried fronts of office buildings (figure 4.3)?

Examining many approaches to design, early and mid-nineteenth-century theorists of ornament such as Augustus Pugin, John Ruskin, and Owen Jones proposed some general principles governing the design and distribution of ornament. Indeed, Jones began his universal theory of ornament with thirty-seven propositions governing color and shape as the basis for conventionalization. Other theorists attempted to formulate rules for convening meaningful figures into new types and technologies of building. The problem was largely one of establishing new systems of visual design, that is, visual "grammars," capable of moving beyond old styles to serve a more complex theater of architectural production.

From their analysis of historical ornaments, such as the lotus and the acanthus (figure 4.4), the Victorians determined that conventionalized figures were generally regularized and simplified away from their natural forms. They were necessarily artificial figures as they became properties of architecture rather than nature, their natural or original configurations having been subordinated to the shapes and forms of their settings. In many cases, their settings, such as walls, were completely flat. The process of conventionalization might have meant exaggerating or eliminating the minor features of a particular leaf or flower, while major features might have been limited to their formal

4.4 The leaves of the conventionalized lotus ornament were regularized and simplified from their natural form.

4.5 Figures of ornament, such as the palmette, were often limited to their abstract outlines.

49

4.6 The human figures on the
west portal of Chartres Cathedral
are pure sculpture.

planar outlines (figure 4.5). By the late nineteenth century, such
design procedures were already considered a form of abstraction.

Most of the nineteenth-century theorists exalted nature, particularly botanical nature, as the most important external source of figuration in ornament. While primitive cultures often distributed simple
geometric shapes and zigzags about objects, the Victorians tended to
treat pure geometry more as a means of organization than as a source
of iconic or particularly meaningful figures. Animal shapes appeared
more as grotesques and objects of humor, while the complete, as com-

50

pared to the fragmented, human figures generally belonged to the art of pure sculpture and tended to be artworks located in the context rather than the line work of ornament (figure 4.6). As a rule, ornamenters abstracted natural objects and regarded literal, or what they termed "naturalized," representations as a form of portraiture.

The historian Edward N. Kaufman, in a study of this concern in Victorian theories of ornament, uses phrases like "shared substance" or "the blending of essences" in his description of the middle ground sought between the external things evoked by ornament and the internal facts of the object or space being ornamented.[23] He emphasizes a third or adjunct condition, essentially formal and often immaterial, into which, for example, an essence of the foliage and an essence of the wall could be positioned. Such a condition involves establishing a set of regulating lines, lineaments, or planes that help define the wall as well as the particular types of foliage that originated apart from the wall. The lines, lineaments, or planes of ornament share some of the geometry common to both the wall per se and the external actions of figures evoked by the ornament. For example, the fleur-de-lis (figure 4.7), distributed as a repeating and commanding ornament on a stone wall, refers in part to an iris but is already a remote representation of a flower, having jettisoned its innate three-dimensionality by becoming flat. In the course of that flattening, some fleurs-de-lis also acquired the character of a dagger in the pointed extension of the central leaf. The rough materiality and physique of the wall must also lose some of their innate stoniness as they convene with the flat fleur-de-lis. The foliage and the stone wall are thus both "imperfected" from their literally natural state as they submit to a flat realm in which only certain residual essences of the originally distinct elements remain visually intelligible. The prolific nineteenth-century architect Sir Gilbert Scott, commenting on this process, characterized the flattening and geometrizing of branches and leaves as "the architecturalization of foliage."[24]

In his chapter "The Nature of Gothic" in *The Stones of Venice*, Ruskin challenged the idea of perfection and unchangeability in the idealization of any figure in design and called, instead, for an amount of servitude between things: "Imperfection is in some sort essential to all that we know of life."[25] He suggested that the craftsperson designing and situating an ornament struggle with all the characters of the foliage and the wall "with as much accuracy as was compatible with the laws of his design and the nature of his material, not [to be] infrequently tempted in his enthusiasm to transgress the one and disguise the other." This seminal call for expressionism as a means of conventionalization real-

4.7 The iris has discarded its innate three-dimensionality by becoming the flat fleur-de-lis.

4.8, 4.9 The ideas of foliation and architectural construction are intertwined in their placement around a window upon the University Museum, Oxford.

ized a passionate approach and a sort of "active rigidity" between elements of design, or what Louis Sullivan was to call "mobile equilibrium."[26]

Ruskin also proposed ways of impressing foliation into the typical forms of building in order to dramatize relations between architecture and nature.

The Corinthian capital is beautiful, because it expands under the abacus just as Nature would have expanded it; and because it looks as if the leaves had one root, though that root is unseen. And the flamboyant leaf moldings are beautiful, because they nestle and run up the hollows, and

fill the angles and clasp the shafts which natural leaves would have delighted to fill and clasp. They are no mere cast of natural leaves; they are counted, orderly, and architectural: but they are *naturally*, and there fore beautifully, placed.[27]

In the University Museum of Natural History in Oxford, designed in 1856 by Benjamin Woodward, some of Ruskin's theories of conventionalization were intentionally realized, perhaps most explicitly in a unique system of composition that combines distinct ideas of foliation and construction by placing them immediately adjacent and parallel to one another around a window (figures 4.8 and 4.9). This curious system was inspired by thirteenth-century Gothic architecture. Note the band of alternating dark and light stones around the perimeter of the arch, the band of foliation running parallel to and immediately underneath the checkered stones, and the band of cylindrical molding that is the archivolt, running immediately underneath the band of foliation. Each of these bands is "convened" into the limited space of the frame of the window, and each represents or evokes a different visual idea. The checkered stones articulate the formal facts of construction, the leaf moldings "run up the hollows" and suggest the rhythms of botanical nature, and the archivolt, like the shaft from which it springs, articulates a classically Gothic ordering of construction rather than the physical facts of construction. All of these "ideas" are compressed within and regulated by the linear margin around the window. The margin provides a space between the crude mass of the wall and the tracery within the window in which distinct visual ideas are combined and regulated by their contiguity and similarity of direction.

Sullivan, who read Ruskin and was familiar with Gothic ornaments through his study at the Beaux-Arts, achieved a strategy that was largely of his own devising. Like Ruskin, he understood the importance of regulating his foliated ornament by subjecting the shapes and locations of the ornament to the geometric authority of the basic architectural form. We might say that Sullivan's strategy of conventionalization was based on a preliminary geometrization of all architectural elements,

4.10 Louis Sullivan began by organizing all the elements of his buildings into geometric units. Wainwright Tomb, St. Louis, 1892.

from the basic shape of the entire building to the marginal spaces in which he planned to distribute ornament. He began by organizing both the overall mass and the subordinate elements of his buildings into simple geometric units and zones (figure 4.10). The dominant volumes were blocklike, and the subordinate elements such as windows and doors were regularly and symmetrically positioned. But after those preliminary moves, he "awakened"[28] the basic geometry within the margins designated for ornament in the direction of natural efflorescence, or flowering. To do this, he elaborated and manipulated small units of geometry, transforming them from rigid polygons into the dynamic and radiant plant forms that constituted his ornaments (figure 4.11). He carried this out in careful design operations in which the outer edges of a polygon, such as a square or pentagon, were multiplied by lines pushing inward as well as outward. He then subdivided and further elaborated the surfaces of the polygons in the direction of organic curves that often wove into lines bursting outward from the center as though the entire figure were exploding. All the time, Sullivan was developing his ornament toward an organic complexity and away from a basic geometric simplicity. His figures were to reflect the spirit of nature, and their foliations thus appeared to burst out of the building material to arouse the entire work of architecture from its most basic geometric torpor. Indeed, Sullivan was able to employ regular geometry as the realm, the flatland, so to speak, in which his efflorescing figures within ornament and his basic expressions of construction could merge and coexist. In a profound way, Sullivan's architecture revealed geometry as an underlying property of all things, from animals and flowers to arches and hinges, and in so doing renewed some of the most ancient and revered practices of conventionalization.

Ornamenters contemporary to Sullivan also employed geometry, although in a design process opposite to Sullivan's. The French designer Victor M. C. Ruprich-Robert, for instance, would select a plant or flower and proceed to manipulate its figure in the direction of Euclidian geometry, rather like some early twentieth-century efforts in painting and sculpture to abstract or simplify images of nature. Ruprich-Robert believed that the plant's "savage form" should be disciplined and regularized by the civilizing inclinations of the human mind. Once civilized, the transformed figure of the plant could be distributed in another geometrically civilized artifice such as a work of architecture.[29]

Ruprich-Robert's discipline included bilateral and dynamic symmetry through the inscribing of regular geometry into a flat botanical

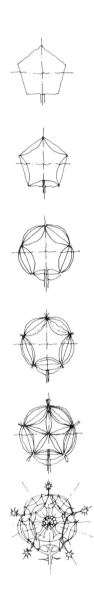

4.11 Sullivan transformed rigid geometric figures into organic, plantlike forms that constituted his ornaments.

*4.12 Ruprich-Robert trans-
formed organic plant forms
into more geometric shapes.*

shape that corresponded to its innate numeration (figure 4.12). Thus
a daffodil, because its floral petals were constituted by a double layer of
three outward-pointing leaves, would be disciplined by the symmetry of
a hexagon. In comparison to Sullivan's process of awakening, we might
call this a process of tranquilizing, in which an organic shape was conventionalized in the direction of a frozen geometric form.

For the Victorian theorists, such as Ruskin, Sullivan, and Ruprich-
Robert, conventionalization was critical to the development of modern
ornament to the extent that the process could visibly combine a range of
expressions about nature, history, and social values into the rational fabric of the new industrialized means of building. Multiple levels and
means of expression could remain an integral property of a modern language of architecture, and architecture could flourish as a rich and
expressive tapestry of meanings. Unlike the early modernists of the twentieth century, who moved to simplify, reduce, and homogenize the elements of design, the Victorians thought of architecture as the mother
art—responsible for the incorporation and nourishment of the entire
family of arts—in which the representational capacities of painting, poly-
chromy, sculpture, symbolic detail, and craft were united through
thoughtful systems of conventionalization (figures 4.13, 4.14, and 4.15).

*4.13 William Butterfield's pulpit is
an example of conventionalized polychrome ornament. All Saints, London.*

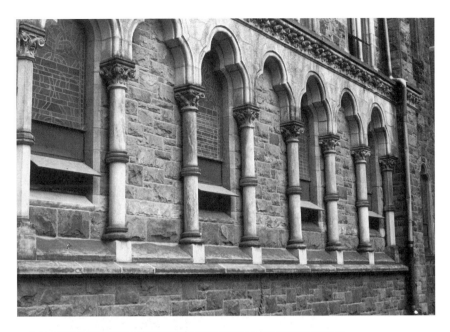

4.14 Russell Sturgis's foliations are incorporated into the facade of the Battell Chapel, Yale University, New Haven.

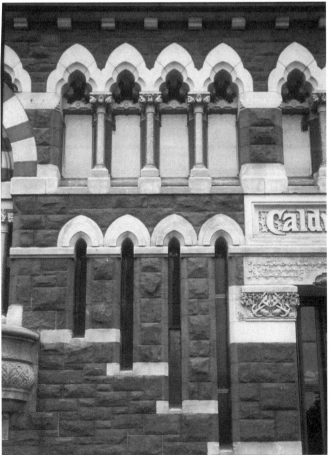

4.15 Steel trusses and conventionalized ornaments rhythmically combine on Edward Potter's Colt Memorial, Hartford.

4.16 The Colt Memorial expresses muscularity in construction unified with delicate evocations of nature.

4.17 Frank Furness's Pennsylvania Academy of Fine Arts also reconciles the sublime and the beautiful.

Although they were interested in expressing the nature and ethos of the society in which their buildings were situated, they understood that diminishing the most basic expressions of construction and space would reduce the power of ornament. They also knew that construction was but one of the themes central to the linguistic potential of architecture.

Indeed, it is difficult to look at the finest examples of Victorian architecture today without sensing the muscularity of the buildings with their dramatic arches, eaves, columns, brackets, and rugged masonry (figures 4.16 and 4.17). Yet at the same time we notice the delicate scrollwork, stained glass, stenciling, and carved wood. There does not seem to be a disjuncture of elements. Such accomplishments depended on thoughtful and rigorous design strategies and the abstraction of natural elements—a combination of the systematic approaches of Victorian theorists and traditional systems inherited from classical and Gothic precedents.

Curiously, however, in their writings about conventionalization the Victorians rarely pointed to one of the most powerful means of combining inherent and adherent figures of expression. They barely discussed the combining power of *rhythm*.

5.1 The regular meter of the windows precedes the irregular rhythm of the ornament. Ronald Reagan National Airport, Washington, D.C.

RHYTHM

Long before writing was invented, even before
parietal writing was practiced, something
was produced which may fundamentally
distinguish man from animal: the intentional
reproduction of a rhythm: there have been
found on cave walls of the Mousterian epoch
certain rhythmic incisions—and everything
suggests that these first rhythmic representations coincide with the appearance of
the first human habitations.

Roland Barthes[30]

The term *rhythm* is both casually used and misused in theories of architectural design, while it is central to discussions about the narrative structure of music and the organization of dance. Visual compositions are generally studied in the province of geometry rather than rhythm. When we analyze the forms of painting, sculpture, and building or the configuration of conventionalized ornament we almost always employ geometry rather than rhythm as our primary means. These customary uses of rhythm and geometry make common sense, especially if we associate rhythm with time, as in music, and geometry with space, as in architecture. Music is overtly temporal, and visual designs, particularly architecture, painting, and sculpture, are more fixed in space, although it would be a mistake to assume that music is without its spatial connotations or that visual design, especially ornament, can flourish without incorporating the affective drives of rhythm. Indeed, rhythm may be the primary organizational feature of ornament, with principles of geometric organization subordinate to it (I discuss this idea in chapters 8 and 9.) We might even conclude that, among the various visual disciplines, ornament manifests the extreme potential of rhythmizing.

But how can the phenomenon of rhythm be incorporated in a composition that is fundamentally fixed in time and may even, like certain sculptures, paintings, and facades, be immediately comprehended in whole cloth as singular objects firmly seated on the ground or fixed upon a wall? Doesn't the overall physical unity of a seated object pervade and control the entire composition? By paying close attention to the ways that we actually look at and examine such an object, we learn that while we can take in the whole object at once, so to say, we also allow our gaze to travel around the surface and survey the details. When we examine a page in a book, likewise, we can either perceive the texture of the entire page or read the text in a serial manner. In addition, the fact that we can do the latter while remaining aware of the former indicates that we can visually engage an object both spatially and temporally at the same time. But the temporal movement of the eye and the sequential examination of detail are not the only ways we engage rhythm in ornament.

An ornament can also *represent* or *manifest* the critical features of rhythm while remaining static in appearance or being perceived as an entire composition. The notion that ornament can represent rhythm demands that we attempt to understand rhythm as a representable phenomenon with specific discernible features, an attempt made difficult by the fact that very little is known about the deepest nature of rhythm. For example, while we intuitively understand the drive of rhythm while listening to jazz, we may struggle to explain the crucial function of rhythm in speech, painting, or ornament. However, our understanding of rhythm may be strengthened if we assume that rhythm is the same basic phenomenon regardless of whether it is perceived as a property of music, dance, speech, painting, or ornament.

In contemporary colloquial usage, rhythm is often incorrectly reduced to the notion of a regular repeat. But musicians, designers, dancers, and scholars seem to agree that the perception of rhythm, and the intentional act of rhythmizing, is not reducible to the kind of periodic repetition produced by a metronome, the alpha discharges of radium, or the sun's rotation. It is a corporeal and mental activity that on one level acknowledges periodic repetition while on another consciously moves to push, pull, syncopate, disrupt, and shift the boredom of regular repetition. It is actually experienced as an irregular pattern.

One interpretation of an ancient Greek meaning proposes: "Rhythm then is that which imposes bonds on movement and confines the flux of things. . . . [R]hythm in music and dancing is not *flow* but *pause*, the steady limitation of movement."[31] For the ancient philosophers, the notion of unlimited motion would have suggested a condition of chaos rather than order (ornament), and hence the discipline of rhythm required "'form, shape,' or 'pattern'"[32] to rescue thought from the abyss of unlimited repetition.

In the course of a dance certain obvious patterns or positions, like the raising or lowering of a foot, were naturally repeated, thus marking intervals in the dance. Since music and singing were synchronized with dancing, the recurrent positions taken by the dancer in the course of his movements also marked distinct intervals in the music. . . . This explains why the basic component of music and poetry was called a . . . "foot" . . . or . . . "step" . . . and why, within the foot, the basic elements were called the . . . "lifting, up-step" and the . . . "placing, downbeat."[33]

Over time, the concept of rhythm became more rational and abstract. Plato regarded rhythm as a mental pattern with less direct reference to physical actions like dancing or marching, although during his time an interest in patterns of speech began to emerge. To the later Greeks and their Western heirs, rhythm became implicated with forms requiring the ordering of movement. In painting and sculpture, visual movement included changes in direction or dimension along curvilinear and enclosing paths within a composition.

Some of the most compelling recent studies of rhythm, especially of the connection between rhythmizing and language, have focused on poetry as the most intentionally rhythmic form of verbal expression. These studies are very useful in our understanding of rhythm in visual language. Indeed, there is an uncanny similarity between the function of rhythm in verbal poetry and its function in visual ornament, even if we grant the material dependency of visual ornament on a particular place. In both cases, pure repetition leads to affective inadequacy and lifelessness: "the ticktock of the pendulum soon becomes monotonous. If a consciousness were to remain within time continuously, it would ultimately annihilate itself—sinking into sleep or catalepsy."[34] Verbal repetition can be compared to a deadly dull chant, while the regular units of visual meter can be understood as a barren geometric grid. The smallest subversion, such as a contraction, the Greek "pause," or a change in pitch, volume, color, location, or orientation, promotes and activates the possibility of a rhythm, which can transform the torpor of regularity into a vital system of memory and the conscious development of complex patterns. Eventually the markings, retentions, and further variations trigger a sense of anticipation or portentiousness. Meanings given to local variations can be structured into the narratives of music and speech or the fabulation of visual ornament. A long sequence might build toward a level of anticipation, then break open into a flourish, an outstanding figure, a collapse, or a climax.

If we allow ourselves to imagine particular phrases and figures as meaningful units of vocabulary to be grammatically ordered in time, we can perceive the basic outline of language itself. Within such a temporal order, there is a syntax in which a sequence of words or a sequence of visual elements is spliced, obscured, stretched, and exclaimed within basic repetitive patterns. Rhythm in this respect may be understood as an aggressive property of design or speech, a driving force, into which both personal and extrapersonal ideas can be invented, gathered, and organized.

As the vocabulary and grammar of both verbal and visual language become more rigidly conventionalized and objectively referential, which is to say more factual than fictional, more denotative than connotive, and thus more rational than poetic, the importance of rhythm is diminished. The reign of consciousness becomes more prescribed, unlike the poetic state in which the individual is inclined to be more united with the social and physical environment in an irrational and fluid state bordering on synaesthesia.

Rhythm may be understood as an extremely fundamental condition that underwrites language from its inception. Julia Kristeva, in her discussion of the "semiotic chora," speaks of rhythm as an essential drive in the ordering of both poetic language and the child's early development of language. She borrows the term *chora* from Plato's *Timaeus* "to denote an essentially mobile and extremely provisional articulation constituted by movements and their ephemeral stases."[35] Her chora is a necessary prelinguistic condition that exists on the verge of articulation and precedes the formation of distinctive marks, words, or figuration. It acts as a receptacle or a space that is periodically expanding and condensing and into which "the subject is both generated and negated . . . as topological spaces that connect the zones of the fragmented body to each other and also to 'external' 'objects' and 'subjects,' which are not yet constituted as such."[36]

For the child, Kristeva's chora is a cauldron into which internal and external cues may ferment before beginning to solidify into the denotative and referential stuff of adult language. It is an unconscious place where

> nothing can be negated, even contradictory forces must dwell together in constant struggle. Kristeva then proposes that these opposing forces are transformed from pure conflict into a kind of rhythmic pulsation by the moderating, stabilizing influence of the chora. The weight of a pendulum works similarly: the pendulum resolves the con-

flicting forces of leftward and rightward swinging into an alternation from left to right, by virtue of its weight.[37]

In due course, the cues become organized in the child's mind and begin to be grammatically structured into intelligible sentences as prototypes of the conventionally rigorous and rational language of adulthood. However, in another stage of life the adult may elect to reenter the receptacle of rhythm in order to juxtapose the very contradictory forces that are separated and crystallized by the necessarily extreme symbolization and denotation of rational language. The receptacle of rhythm and its manifestations in poetry and ornament remain available as a place in which conflict, opposition, or routine differences may be repositioned and recombined into an unbroken spectacle of the open imagining and movement provided by the rhythmic drive.

In some respects, rhythm is an "expression of the principle of equivalence as it is played out across time, along the axis of combination."[38] Moreover, the axial principle of combining in ornament (as in poetry) controls the opposing element on either side of the axis in such a way that sensible things, prior to their admission into ornament, become playful figures of nonsense within the space of ornament, albeit a nonsense mobilized to "undermine the provinciality of the day's values by encouraging a larger, more timeless view of them."[39] Indeed, by incorporating facts of utility into the playful figuration of ornament, ordinary things become enlivened. They become a property of chanting. Practical elements combined with elements from the larger world become enchanted, as they are turned into metaphors within a seamless dreamscape. Within such a rhythmic world, metamorphoses are superadded to the ordinary taxonomy of nature—as we will see in the next chapter, by examining one of ornament's most extraordinary legacies, the invention and development of the epic rhythmized motif that we may identify as the "foliated scroll."

6.1 An Egyptian funerary ornament anticipates the formulation of the classical foliated scroll. Thebes, 7th century B.C.

RHYTHMIZED FOLIATION

Where everything is in flux and nothing
could ever be predicted, habit establishes
a frame of reference against which we can
plot the variety of experience.

Ernst Gombrich[40]

What I shall term the "foliated scroll" has been an indispensable subject for pattern books and theories of ornament over the last 150 years. While the foliated scroll is not the only rhythmized motif in the history of Western ornament, it is certainly the outstanding one in its capacity to provide critical insight into the way that ornament is served by rhythm. It illustrates the wonderful mutations and narratives that a rhythmized system of visual design can produce over time, and as such it has become an indispensable chronicle of composition in the history of Western ornament. It would be difficult to understand the persistent and typical character of ornament without a close look at a basic configuration that has persisted for thousands of years with seemingly infinite variation.

Although ornament is dependent upon utilitarian form and the materials are critical to the particular shaping of practical objects such as columns, bowls, and hats, materials have not played a primary role in the formulation and evolution of the foliated scroll. Specific materials have been responsible for the way that certain motifs have been detailed, and hence a painted acanthus leaf on a Greek wall is shaped quite differently from a carved acanthus leaf in a Roman frieze. A spiral woven from cotton is distinct from a spiral etched into bronze. These distinctions result in part from processes of conventionalization. But the fundamental rhythms, narratives, and fantasias that issue from the foliated scroll seem to have visual lives of their own, which can be manifested in a wide range of materials. Foliated scrolls are usually distributed in the narrow margins between things.

I am using the term *foliated scroll* provisionally to classify a motif that has been given a variety of names. Alois Reigl, the founder of the modern history of ornament, called it "vegetal ornament," "tendril ornament," and "Arabesque." In French classicism, the term *rinceau* describes a leafing form of scrollwork. Owen Jones and Albert Racinet documented the presence of foliated line work in the majority of illustrations included in their great compendiums of world ornament. More recently, Ernst Gombrich picked out the acanthus scroll as the most persistent motif in the history of ornament. The acanthus is a particular leaf that the ancient Greeks conventionalized as one of their most significant botanical figures. In most classical designs, it appears to grow out of or along the axis of a scrolling line work, and therefore we can say that the acanthus scroll is a particular variation of the foliated scroll. Depending on the tightness of the definition, the scroll has a life span of twenty-five hundred to four thousand years and flourished in Europe, North Africa, the Middle East, India, China, and the Americas.

By all accounts, it was born in North Africa and the Middle East and reached its mature formulation in sixth-century B.C. Greece. The principal features of that formulation were:

1. a repetitive or recycling linear wave action;
2. the periodic formation of a scroll shape; and
3. the periodic emergence of a radiating or dilating figure emerging from the scroll that is usually, but not always, conventionalized from plant forms, hence the term *foliation.*

The origin of the classical foliated scroll can be traced from the eighteenth dynasty of Egypt in the sixteenth century B.C. through Crete to Mycenaean pottery in the seventh century B.C. An early example for this period of development may be found in Egyptian funerary ornament at Thebes (figure 6.1). The Egyptian solar motif runs along the bottom of the composition as a cosmic force rising upward out of the ocean. It displays cycles of opening and closing as it produces an expansive radiance and moments of efflorescence. The band of ornament includes a simple repeating row of the lotus bud and the lotus flower (figure 6.2). Although the design illustrates a periodic bud-bloom, it does not graphically represent rotation or movement along an axis. Although the buds and blossoms are threaded together, the

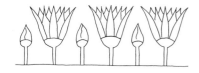

6.2 The Theban funerary relief is ornamented with the simple sequence of bud and lotus flower.

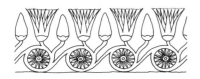

6.3 The bud-and-blossom row is expanded upon by an added hint of rotation in the wheels below the lotus flowers.

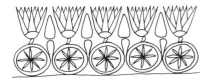

6.4 Here the buds have their own point of origin between the circles.

6.5 The lotus blossoms are separate from their buds, which originate between the wheels.

composition is staccato and the figures point only upward. In figure 6.3, a rotating cycle is hinted at by the threaded wheels below the lotuses and the plan of the lotus situated within each circle. This is a dynamic precursor of the foliated scroll, rendered somewhat awkward by the bud and blossom growing from the same point.

In other friezes from wall paintings, the bud and the blossom have their own points of origin—in figure 6.4 between the circles and in figure 6.5 atop the circles. However, no curving lines organically thread the circles together.

In figures 6.6 and 6.7, a scroll threads the plans and the elevations of lotus plants together. All the attributes of the foliated scroll are assembled into a rolling wavelike action, and we might regard this pattern as the seminal foliated scroll were it not for the extremely tight packing of its basic elements. The lotus does not grow out of the coiling line work, but is merely inscribed within the leftover space at the cusps inside the line work. Some scholars have even argued that the Egyptian scroll is not really a scroll in the sense of a tendril freely raveling, but is rather the circumscribed interlock of two geometric coils. Either way, it falls short of what Reigl regarded as the classical formulation of the foliated scroll, because of its graphic inflexibility and the subjugation of its parts to a governing cellular pattern.

The Assyrian ornaments from Nimrud (figures 6.8 and 6.9) owe much to Egyptian precedent, but manage to introduce some important organic line work of their own. In figure 6.8, the ornament connects a narrative of palmette-bud-palmette-flower-palmette-bud with straight, ropelike threads. The two rows are symmetrically aligned on either side of a channel containing a guilloche, or interlace of semicircular waves. Positioned on the axis of the pattern, the guilloche pulsates and cycles, and its focal points are aligned along the spring points of the buds and blossoms. However, the guilloche moves in a channel by itself, apart from the bottoms of the palmettes, buds, and flowers, even as it registers a directional movement for the entire formation along an axis of translation. It lacks integration with the foliation. The connective threads in figure 6.9 curve upward from a base line to a row of circles holding lotuses. The arcs contribute to the springing of the lotuses, but they fail to articulate a cycling movement or to establish a direction of translation. To confer directionality, arrowheads located in the registers along the border and within the arcs point to the right and lend the composition a directional movement.

The border pattern on the alabaster doorsill of an Assyrian palace (figure 6.10) appears to be taken from Egypt because of the lotus-plus-

6.6 The lotus plan and elevation are woven together by a repeating scroll.

6.7 Repeating scrolls form a two-dimensional pattern.

6.8 A ropelike thread connects an Assyrian ornamental sequence of palmette-bud-palmette-flower-palmette-bud.

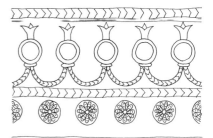

6.9 In this sequence the lotuses are threaded together by a string of arcs.

6.10 An Assyrian doorsill border resembles the Egyptian lotus-bud pattern.

6.11 The Tree of Assyria is composed of a "trunk" connecting a sequence of palmettes together in an upright composition.

6.12 A Mycenean vase design consists of undulating lines resembling ivy and an octopus.

bud pattern. Its contemporary, the Tree of Assyria (figure 6.11), connects palmettes together as they surround a "tree trunk" sprouting a palmette at its crown. The composition is guided by the idea of a tree that is far from a literal representation. The trunk itself is arrowed upward in the direction of its growth. This decoratively banded trunk seems to borrow some of the attributes of the earlier motifs, as lateral supports reach out to the foliations running around the perimeter.

Certain features of what was to become the mature foliated scroll were developed by a variety of nations on and around the Aegean peninsula that were connected by trade routes. A more natural undulating line, for example, which Alois Reigl was to call a botanic "tendril," seems to be a necessary precursor. The tendril allowed a variety of connections and freedoms of movement previously locked into much more rigid patterns. The design on a Mycenaean vase (figure 6.12) features a foliated, undulating line amidst curious wiggles and spirals floating in the surrounding space. Bisymmetrical scrolls appear at the bottom of each ivy leaf, and rotating tendril scrolls appear as the legs of octopus shapes casually swimming around. From the same period, a literal version of the octopus appears in a teacup from Dendra (figure 6.13) on the island of Crete. The central undulating line in the Mycenaean design is a visual element in its own right, although it appears to function as the parent stem of a row of leaves with small rows of three and four tendrils growing left and right from the axis. Thus the undulating line and the tendrils allude to forms in nature while being constituted by a rather abstract system of artificial line work. Indeed, the Mediterranean artisans were formulating a distinct system of ornament capable of evoking rhythm and incorporating a larger variety of motifs gathered from the natural world. In the fifth century B.C., the Greeks refined these precedents, or etymologies, of line work into combinations that are less organic and natural than those of either Mycenaean or Minoan ornament but much more elegantly organized and liberated from the patterns of stiff geometry found in the Egyptian. By rendering the figures of plant and spiral as distinct elements and by distributing them within an undulating wave pattern, the Greeks were able to finally formulate the foliated scroll as a fully conventional system.

Riegl saw the border of a Melian amphora (figure 6.14) as marking the moment just preceding the mature foliated scroll, and he pointed to the emerging figural autonomy of the scroll in the Melian example. The Melian scrolls tilt up and down in the space between the lotus forms that articulates the overall form of an undulating wave. The scroll thus rendered as the end of a tendril becomes, in Riegl's words, an "intermittent tendril" capable of greater rhythmic and geometric variation.

Let me digress for a moment from the story of the foliated scroll to propose that the spiral is the most generative figure in the history of ornament. Showing up in the ornament of all cultures, it speaks of virtual energy. It is also one of the most convenient shapes for visually articulating the actions of continuous dilation and contraction. As an elegant geometric figure in its own right, the spiral is universally recognizable. The mind seems to readily accept the spiral as standing alone or as belonging to the beginning or end of a larger system of line work. It is readily capable of unwinding or rewinding along a repeating pathway. As a sort of elastic geometry, the spiral adapts and transforms itself in the presence of other things and actions; it is unsurpassed as an element of fluid and dynamic movement. It is curious, then, that the spiral has nearly vanished in the compositions of modern art that exist apart from a dependence on the expression of utilitarian things, whereas it seems to readily combine with the surfaces of practical objects.

The lines of the Greek scrolls freely explore space, functioning now and then as catalysts of radiant figures. The tendrils in an Attic bowl (figure 6.15) grip the lotus figure in the Egyptian manner while simultaneously interlacing, waving, and producing spiral endings. The flip-flopping lotuses in figure 6.16 are connected by stems aspiring to be scrolls, while the double-ended scrolls in figure 6.17 are fully devel-

6.13 A more literal figure of an octopus appears on a copper cup from Dendra.

6.14 The design on a Melian amphora produces a scroll, shown on the left side of this drawing.

6.15 The Greek scrolls on an Attic bowl grip the lotus flowers, filling the border space.

6.16 Threads that are almost scrolls connect the pattern of flip-flopping lotuses.

6.17 Independent scrolls like intermittent tendrils connect the lotuses and palmettes.

6.18 Palmettes and lotuses radiate upward from the wave action of the tendrils running along the bottom.

6.19 The large intermediate coil, reminiscent of the ancient Egyptian model, interrupts a flip-flopping lotus motif.

6.20 Tendrils roam freely along the surface of a Greek bowl.

6.21 The pattern on the neck of a Greek vase generates animals leaping outward into space.

oped figures performing full wave action and triggering the radiations of upward palmettes and downward lotuses. The psychological energy implicit in the waves and flip-flops inspires the mind to both retain old motions and predict any number of future motions. Such retention and prediction fuel the emergence of ever new life-forms, shapes, or symbols. Indeed, so energetic a formulation epitomizes the visual shape of linear rhythm.

In figure 6.18, the wave action of the scrolls drops to the bottom of the band, allowing the palmettes and lotuses to radiate upward. In a pattern from the Temple of Jupiter (figure 6.19), the basic wave is achieved by flip-flopping the lotus motif while creating a large intermediate interlocking coil reminiscent of the ancient Egyptian motif.

In the handle of a Greek bowl (figure 6.20), the tendril lines roam freely over the surface to generate three figures: the palmettes efflorescing from small bisymmetrical pairs of volutes, a seedlike lotus, and leaves at the tips. In the space of a neck ornament taken from a vase (figure 6.21) tendrils issue palmettes, lotuses, polyps, budlike forms, scrolls, and even animals, which leap outward from the spaces harbored between.

The evocative gestural line work within these rhythmized examples of classical Greek ornament reveals the eloquence of the foliated scroll and provides a glimpse of those mechanisms that allow it to apprehend, gather, invent, and manifest the curious inhabitants within the world of ornament.

After the Greek formulation, the foliated scroll began to travel around the world, apprehending new figures and producing new rhythms along the way. As the Alexandrian conquests expanded eastward, so did the architecture and artifacts of Hellenistic society. Grecian buildings occupied the land of today's Syria, Iraq, Jordan, Turkey, Iran, Afghanistan, and the Punjab. Grecian ornamented artifacts were traded throughout Central Asia. After the final conquest and expulsion of the Greeks in the second century B.C., the Parthians, near northern Iran, and Kushans, within present-day Pakistan, occupied their standing cities and savored the details of Greek ornament.

Jessica Rawson, in *Chinese Ornament*, offers an explanation of the means by which the foliated scroll moved from the borders of Greek temples into similar spaces upon the elevations of Buddhist cave temples. In the late stages of Greek architecture, upright statues of important men were generally located between the columns of Greek monuments, theaters, and tombs, with scrolls running along the entablatures over their heads. Those enshrined figures, placed there for political and didactic purposes, were exalted by their presence within the architecture. When the early Buddhists adopted some of the elements in Greek architecture for their temples, they placed Buddhas between the columns and appropriated the scrolls. The scrolls that prevailed in the early years of their adoption were crude compared to the Greek prototype, but they still contained the genetics needed to fuel a powerful Asian excursus.

A stone relief from a second- to third-century A.D. Buddhist cave temple in Gandhara (figure 6.22) has a simple wave stem sprouting partial scrolls efflorescing into half-palmettes. Asian artisans adopted the half-palmette, perhaps because it has a vivid thrusting action that, when repeated, punctuates the direction of translation. The minimal arrangement of wave and half-palmette that migrated into China, as Rawson points out, was sufficient to perpetuate the foliated scroll and to nourish the development of elaborate flower patterns that were uniquely Chinese.

Chinese artisans, abandoning the rigorous symmetry and geometry of the Greek palmette, dynamically rotated the half-palmette into a fan shape growing out of a joint along the wavy stem (figure 6.23). This elegant radiation features a miniature cluster of scrolls sprouting from its base. Like the alternating Egyptian sequence of bud-blossom-bud, this motif beats out a rhythm of seed-fan-seed. This bisymmetrical motif is a composite form in which a stem issues a seed from which another stem emerges surrounded with smaller leaves. On either side of the newly sprouted plant figure, slightly detached scrolls trail off into space, plumes of vapor reminiscent of Asian cloud motifs. In subsequent designs, such clouds seem to assert themselves and demand their own sky (figure 6.24) in the turbulence of a rather free and calligraphic composition. The ancient Greek forms from which these ornaments were descended were giving way to a lyrical Chinese portrayal of elegance and energy.

After the tips of blossom shapes, originally derived from the palmette and the lotus, dissolved into clouds, the blossom itself was transformed into a peony (figures 6.25 and 6.26). With its intricate lines and abundant petals, the peony evoked palatial luxury and sexuality, and became the preferred flower of the imperial T'ang household in the eighth century, whereas the lotus motif, representing a subordinate religious group, was rejected by the court. By the eleventh century, the dominant motif consisted of a peony forming, billowing around the axis of the wavy line, and emitting clouds from its tips. The cloud motif as the climax of a flower may be enigmatic to the Western eye; it is

6.22 A wave stem, from a Buddhist cave temple, sprouts half-formed palmettes.

6.23 The half-palmette was transformed into a fan in the Chinese tradition.

6.24 The scrolls are detached and trail off, while the clouds assert themselves within the pattern.

6.25, 6.26 As the lotus dissolves into a cloud, the blossom is transformed into a peony.

6.27 An accomplishment of the Ming dynasty was the rediscovery of the lotus flower as a decorative motif.

6.28 Chinese motifs were transmitted back to the West through the borders of Persian miniatures.

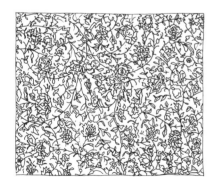

6.29 The Chinese influence is seen in the labyrinthine surfaces of Iranian carpets. Iran, 16th century.

absent from our own repertoire of conventionalized ornament. Such representations of wispy cloud tendrils are conventionalized figures of Chinese ornament, however, derived from observations of vapor pushing out of a cloud into the prowlike or spearlike leading edge of its motion. The hybrid form of cloud-flowers was first employed in foliated scrolls by the artisans of the Liao dynasty in the fourth century A.D. Although the Chinese thus introduced the cloud and peony motifs, their craftspeople never fully abandoned the seminal lotus. Both the peony and the lotus thrive in Chinese gardens, content, so to say, to be associated with waves, tendrils, and scrolls.

In the ensuing centuries, the foliated scroll and its particular geometries maintained an inherent authority capable of renewing itself. By the fourteenth century, the lotus had reappeared as the principal motif on a foliated scroll (figure 6.27), contributing to the elegance of the great Ming accomplishment. The ancient lotus motif has pointed tips, and the Asian peony motif has rounded tips. The Ming flowers seem to be peony-lotuses, or perhaps their pointed petals are hybridized with clouds. The vine revolving about the flowers is sprouting scrolls as well as scrolls issuing clouds that seem to be leaves, and thus an illusion of natural vining is also a semblance of spiraling wind. This artifice derived from nature is a marvel of composition; such Ming transformations of the Greek formula benefited from a thousand years of speculation inside China. In many ways, the Ming scroll is more sensual and spectacular than its Greek precedents, although it is not as well suited to buildings as it is to ceramics and textiles, perhaps because of its extreme delicacy, intricacy, and intimacy.

The powerful Chinese motifs and grammar sustained an afterlife of their own. Transmitted back to the West on porcelain exported along the Silk Road, the delicate line work of the Ming scroll found a new spatial frontier along the borders of miniature Persian paintings in the fifteenth century (figure 6.28) and within the labyrinthine surfaces of sixteenth-century Iranian carpets (figure 6.29).

The incorporation of the foliated scroll into Chinese ornament probably benefited from the fact that Chinese art had previously reached a level of formal articulation and systemization similar in some respects to the Greeks. The basic graphic system governing the Greek formula consisted of a repetitive linear wave, the periodic formation of a scroll shape, and the distribution of radiant plant forms. The Chinese had mastered all three "actions" before the advent of Buddhism in China—except that the dragon, rather than the lotus, was the primary representational motif. In a ritual jade disk from late Eastern Chou in the third century B.C. (figure 6.30), the wave, scroll, and dragon parts are brilliantly intertwined. Much earlier, in a Western Chou disc from the period 1172–722 B.C. (figure 6.31), the first two attributes are present without literal representations of animal parts. Both discs possess the lively representations of rhythm distributed along the edges that we observed in the Greek examples.

The ancient ornament of all great cultures began with geometric motifs, followed by animal motifs and, by virtue of the Mediterranean vision, botanical motifs. Zoomorphic forms such as dragons flourished in ancient Scandinavia, and dragonlike serpents appeared in the ceramics belonging to the isolated ancient cultures of Meso-America. The Mediterranean accomplishment in the first millennium B.C., therefore, was the introduction of rooted and leafing forms as the principal figures from nature to be placed in consonance with a translating system of line work. That line work was abstract in form, although Reigl identified it as evoking tendrils. Moreover, the Western formulation of the foliated scroll allowed a subsequent incorporation of figuration derived from animals, humans, stars, geometry, and all manner of culturally specific trivia.

Periodic ornament alluding to foliation appears to allow a greater number, or at least a more efficient number, of figural moves than ornament alluding only to animals. Two-dimensional abstractions of animal forms are more likely to produce rather simple and unified shapes possessing only heads, tails, and limbs, whereas plant forms, especially in two dimensions, offer more complex branching and more spectacular and multiple lines of radiation and profusion. In other words, flat plants are more mathematically complex and variable than flat animals. In addition, plant forms, both in design and in nature, seem to suggest the environment or the natural surround more than does the centered objecthood of the animal, which we see as moving *inside* an environment. And the annual cycles of renewal in the plant world are easier to articulate in ornament (such as through the bud and the blossom) than are the extended birth-and-death cycles of animals.

The expressive power of the foliated scroll flourished in the West as well, as another afterlife of the ancient world began in the homeland of its local conquerors. At the same time that the motif was migrating eastward toward China, the foliated scroll moved westward into Roman and Greco-Roman architecture and artifacts. For the next two thousand years, the cultural centers of the Western and Near-Eastern worlds were not as stable as the imperial center of China had been, and, perhaps as a consequence, the rhythms of the Western scroll apprehend-

6.30 The Chinese elements of wave, scroll, and dragon are intertwined on this jade disk. Eastern Chou, 3rd century B.C.

6.31 This disk is a lively representation of rhythm in ancient ornament. Eastern Chou, 1172–722 B.C.

6.32 Clothed in foliage, the spine of the scroll becomes more visceral.

6.33 Greco-Roman ornament draped the intermittent tendril in leafage.

6.34 The Romans developed a florid species of foliation.

6.35 In the absence of the lotus, winged persons and geometry emerge from the scrolls. Pompeii.

6.36 Scrolling stalks converge to make a trefoil. Byzantine.

ed and manifested a virtual madhouse of ornament, issuing all manner of fantastic creatures and mutations.

The graphic elegance of the seminal Greek version was remarkable, especially in the balance between conventionalized elements and their adjacent space, or, we might say, between figures and their grounds. Each element, whether it was a scroll or the parts of a lotus or palmette, was individuated into succinct visual forms. Small elements were assembled into larger pieces, like the seven water-drop shapes within the palmette that together form a coherent overall shape (see figure 6.17). The tendril was often a pure line work in its own right with precise geometrically spiraling terminals. Evidently, the classical Greek eye required a sense of balance and a careful control of harmony throughout, as though to civilize the motif by denying its original savage shape.

In time, this magical equivalence between figure and ground gave way to a focus on the materiality of the elements within the foliated scroll. Instead of being conventionalized into elegant graphic shapes, the foliation became more visceral and natural in the hands of late Greek and early Roman carvers. They treated the scroll more three-dimensionally and broke up its continuous lines into stalks, one sprouting from the axis of another (figure 6.32). In figure 6.33, the shapes descended from the classical Greek flip-flopping lotus and palmette scroll are still intact and clearly visible, while the spine of the scroll has become engulfed in the more literally botanical foliage of an acanthus leaf. In Rome, the native acanthus replaced the lotus adapted by the ancient Egyptians as their dominant element of foliation. (Curiously, the lotus survived longer in China and the Far East.) Like the Mycenaean tendril, the more sculptural Roman ornament mimicked nature and apprehended the world of botany in a fantastical new way as it developed into an exuberant and florid type of expression (figure 6.34).

In the polychrome flat patterns of Pompeii, perhaps refined by Greek artisans, the basic line work retained an amount of geometric coherence while managing to incorporate griffins or winged horses into the axes of the scrolls. In an adjacent cycle, geometric shapes sprout where there might have been a lotus (figure 6.35).

On the frieze of a church in Constantinople (figure 6.36), Byzantine carvers once again elaborated the ancient line work by subdividing the powerful waves into bundles of stalks terminating in pointed tips. The tips appear to be leaves, which converge in the center of the semicircular space to articulate the outline of a trefoil inscribed by deep cutouts. This turbulent frieze proposes a tension between the trefoil and the bundles of stalks from which they issue.

Forces radiating from the troughs, crests, and spaces of the foliated scroll may drive inward like the tips of the Byzantine leaves or leap and reach outward like the wings of the griffins from Pompeii. Within the same undulating pathway the forces can drive inward at one interval and drive outward at another. Those movements, expansions, and contractions are rhythmized gestures searching for poetic content. They are the basic grammar of a visual language constituted to gather and to fold extraordinary things into the architecture of ordinary things.

Sometimes the juxtaposition of the ordinary and the extraordinary is achieved by placing more literal elements in unusual places. The animals within the vortexes of Coptic scrolls, for example, have been captured (figure 6.37). They are surprised and denied their customary movements as the spiraling foliation acts to rotate their bodies, while their ears and the engulfing leaves become wrought from identical geometries. A powerful and semicircular wave action moves to the right, punctuated by foliated branches. Miniature scrolls issue from the joints.

Within the frieze above the circular window of an eleventh-century Italian church, a simple wave sprouts half-palmettes from its scrolling branches (figure 6.38). Its organization is identical to the wave and half-palmettes copied by the Buddhists in the second- and third-century cave temples (see figure 6.22). Here, five-pointed leaves and some grapes appear as entourage to the curious animals nesting within alternating cells. The animals neither emerge directly from the tendrils and cusps like the Pompeiian creatures in figure 6.35 nor struggle within the circular Coptic coils but simply relax and dwell in niches upon platforms created by the waves. Yet as winged animals that do not exist in the natural world, they dwell comfortably in a similarly make-believe world that is their artificial habitat.

The axial branch or continuous stem with its stumps functions as a rather literal figure issuing florid leaves (figure 6.39) that curve back and reorganize into waves and scrolls. This ornament expresses a realism typical of the thirteenth-century Gothic carvers and is much more natural than the tendrils of antiquity, despite the fact that this botanic figure is not derived from any obvious plant form. A similar conventionalized realism appears in the carved line work and leaves of a foliated scroll in a medieval frieze in Notre-Dame de Paris (figure 6.40), yet here the ancient superstructure of wave, scroll, and radiation is intact. While owing some of their shape to watercress, the leaves are also the architectural inventions of superb craftspeople. The thir-

6.37 The more literal forms of the animals have been captured within the vortices of the foliated scrolls. Coptic.

6.38 Curious animals nestle in the spaces created by the wave and half-palmette pattern on this frieze. Italy, 11th century.

6.39 An axial branch issues florid leaves that swirl into a scroll formation on this Gothic carving. Medieval Germany, 14th century.

6.40 More conventionalized plants are rendered within the ancient form of wave and scroll. Notre-Dame de Paris.

6.41 A beautiful scroll composition by Mantegna. Italy, 15th century.

6.42 Mantegna's "Battle of the Sea Gods."

6.43 Inspired by Mantegna, this composition by Vico includes monsters generating from foliated tissue.

6.44 Contained within the atmosphere created by the scrolls, the literal cupids behave with an amount of independence.

teenth-century Gothic foliated scroll is a dialect of the classical root, although the craftspeople of that period did not limit their elements of foliation to such highly conventionalized figures as the lotus and the acanthus. Indeed, they searched the garden, field, and forest for a much larger menu of botanical elements ranging from branches and oak leaves to thorns and berries. Natural life-forms within the Gothic architecture became encyclopedic in the thirteenth century. The late Gothic ornament in northern Europe bore less and less resemblance to its roots in Greco-Roman classicism.

At the beginning of the Renaissance, the Italians began in earnest to revive and excavate the old Roman ornaments and at first proceeded to copy the Roman artifacts. By the early sixteenth century, they began to imagine new possibilities for the foliated scroll. Master painters and printmakers made delicate, beautiful compositions, like the scroll (figure 6.41), or *rinceau* (as attributes of the pattern are described in French), which possibly was designed by Andrea Mantegna to embellish one of his own paintings. Enea Vico, meanwhile, engraved horrific sea monsters derived from paintings like Mantegna's *The Battle of the Sea Gods* (figure 6.42). Taken from autonomous paintings and incorporated into the turbulence of the old formula, faces and bodies metamorphose into leaves, fish into calyxes sprouting from tendrils and foliation.

Vico found ways to generate his metamorphic monsters from within the foliated tissue (figure 6.43) of a rinceau that is a fragment of the repeating scroll unregulated by a continuing wave action. Placed in central locations, the line work of a rinceau might move in right- and left-hand pathways issuing from a central figure such as the sea god, only to terminate after a cycle or two. The combinational activity within Vico's space is worth examining carefully as an instance of extraordinarily plastic or organic moments of transformation.

A frieze from a French tomb (figure 6.44) proposes another dimension of metamorphosis, in which the stony substance of the tomb is dissolved and rhythmized into a plasma or an atmosphere. Very shallow, delicate, and flat scrolls emerge slightly above the flat ground. Bulbous sprouts protrude like leaves out of the stem and constellate in the airy space adjacent to the line work, to become sensual things in a realm of space well suited to occupancy by cupids. The literal cupids behave with an amount of independence, although those winged creatures do not seem to desire escape from their fantastic home.

Rhythmized foliation flourished in the French Renaissance palaces of Louis XIV. The court painter Le Pautre understood the joy, the sensuality, and even the terror of the great formula (figure 6.45). Again the potential of the classical foliated scroll is evident as, here, it reflects the voluptuous life of the seventeenth-century French court. Multiple figures from mythology engage in all sorts of behavior, from emerging out of flowers to arriving from beyond the picture frame. The foliation is an environment transforming into the substance of sensual occupants dwelling in a dreamscape, into which all manner of activity is admitted. In this dream, earthly habitation dissolves and is replaced by the sheer rhythmic motion of bodies. In a work of choreography, satyrs mimic the bisymmetry of the joint between waves, while lovers assume asymmetrical postures of embrace.

The spectacular eighteenth-century achievements of rococo ornament began with the momentum of the foliated scroll as a precedent and a resource. Invented on paper in the studios of lithographers and distributed in cartouches along the boundaries of paintings, wall paneling, and the friezes of great rooms, rococo ornament flourished as a subordinate element of architecture. It broke stride with classical regularity by its strident intoxication with asymmetry (figure 6.46), and it called attention to a fantastic realm. It was powerful and exciting, and in certain settings, like the Amelienburg, Spiegelsaal, and the Munich Residenz (figures 6.47 and 6.48), it transported entire rooms into foliated dreamscapes.

With the cast iron of the industrial nineteenth century, the foliated scroll's malleable line work was expressed throughout the world in

6.45 Employing the great formula, Le Pautre portrays the physical bodies of figures dwelling within a dreamscape. France, 17th century.

6.46 The rococo foliated scroll broke with the classical tradition in its strident intoxication with asymmetry.

6.47, 6.48 Exploiting the energy of the ancient foliated scroll, the rocaille transformed entire rooms into arcadian dreamscapes.

6.49 In Labrouste's Bibliothèque Sainte-Geneviève, the rhythmic cycles occupy the ceiling. Paris, 19th century.

railings, fences, trellises, and even trusswork. In the ironwork that supports the ceiling of Labrouste's Bibliothèque in Paris (figure 6.49), for example, the cycles of ornament occupy the upper boundary of a great room. Waves and scrolls in figure 6.50 seem to run up a staircase with an exuberance that produces a sequence of one major and one minor leaf per cycle. On another staircase, a griffin stands guard as a sculptural newel, tailed by a flat and leafy scroll producing extraordinary flowers (figure 6.51).

Nineteenth-century theorists of ornament adapted the formula to the production of printed ornament subject to the graphic tools of the draftsperson. In London, Christopher Dresser's designs were published in pattern books for anyone to purchase. In one (figure 6.52), there is a curiously mechanical interlocking of conventionalized leaves, tendrils, and scrolls, as though in homage to the machine age.

It is important to discuss the history of the foliated scroll, or any ornament, within particular contexts and together with the objects of ornamentation. The preceding examples had particular homes ranging from ancient underground tombs to ceramics and stone walls to the friezes and ceiling trusses of buildings. To conclude this discussion, I will examine a great building from top to bottom and see how ornament fits into its overall scheme. My example will be the St. Louis Wainwright Building, by Adler and Sullivan (1890–91), an important prototype of the tall office building. It seems an appropriate choice because it is a modern building topped off with a brilliant excursus of the foliated scroll, and because many would agree that Louis Sullivan was the greatest ornamenter in American architectural history. Sullivan was able to grammatically unite the foliated scroll (figure 6.53) with the elements of a new architectural form in the process of being invented. In "The Tall Office Building Artistically Considered," an article written five years after the Wainwright was completed, Sullivan reflected upon the hierarchy of essential functions and spaces inherent to a ten-story office building and coined his famous dictum "that *form ever follow function. This is the law.*"[41] With respect to the architecture of the Wainwright Building, Sullivan clearly intended ornament to be an essential part of what he meant by *form,* a term later usurped by theorists who attempted to reduce the meaning of functional form only to articles of practicality and efficiency.

Immediately following these declarations, Sullivan elaborated upon his use of the term by stating that "shape, form, outward expression, design, or whatever we may choose of the tall office building should in the very nature of things follow the functions of the building." The building wanted

> first, a story below ground containing . . . a plant for power, . . . second, a ground floor . . . devoted to stores, banks, or other establishments requiring large area, ample spacing, ample light, and great freedom of access. Third, a second story readily accessible by stairways—this space usually in large subdivisions, with corresponding liberality in structural spacing and expanse of glass and breadth of external opening. Fourth, above this an indefinite number of stories of offices piled tier upon tier . . . an office being similar to a cell in a honeycomb, merely a com-

6.50 Waves and scrolls seem to run up a staircase. U.S., 19th century.

6.51 A griffin stands at the head of a staircase and tails into a leafy scroll. U.S., 19th century.

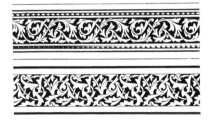

6.52 Published in pattern books, this printed ornament by Christopher Dresser displays a curiously mechanical interlocking of leaves. England, 19th century.

partment, nothing more. Fifth, and last, at the top of this pile is placed a space or story that, as related to the life and usefulness of the structure, is purely physiological in its nature—namely the attic.[42]

Here we have an expression of taut firmness at the bottom, an expression of efflorescence and ornament at the top. As the art historian William Jordy observed, the cladding material itself sets the stage for the emergence of ornaments upon the attic.

> Smooth-surfaced granite provides a base from which smooth-surfaced red brick piers rise to the cornice. . . . By contrast, most of the ornament [upon the attic] appears in terra-cotta, a baked clay which readily receives embellishment in its original ductile state.[43]

In a commanding expression, the building in its entirety articulates the metamorphosis of an upward awakening, of which the foliated scroll is the outer limit and the climax. It is appropriate that the figure located at the center of each cycle is a circular attic window.

From ancient Egypt to the Wainwright Building, the foliated scroll has persisted and functioned as a level of articulation within the greater language of architecture for thousands of years. Its extraordinary life span disputes those claims that would make ornament understandable only in very specific cultural terms rather than in more universal terms, in which it may be understood as a basic form of expression. Indeed, a study of the foliated scroll reveals that it is founded upon a system of visual rhythm in which waving and scrolling line work governs the energy implicit in a collection of abstract figures alluding to foliage. It is a jazzlike system that has produced an extraordinary variety of gestures, visual explosions and implosions, exclamations and surprises. But it is more than the manifestation of raw rhythm. It is a visual means into which figments of our personal and collective imaginations are invited, with permission to scatter and recombine into the uncanny metamorphoses that occupy a special level of human thought.

6.53 Sullivan united the classical elements of the foliated scroll and the modern components of an office building by centering the scrolls around circular windows. Detail of attic frieze, Wainwright Building, St. Louis, 1890–91.

7.1 A keystone trans-
forms into a head in
the company of earthly
sculpture.

METAMORPHOSIS

Ornament—the chosen home of metamorphoses—has given birth to an entire flora and
fauna of hybrids that are subject to the laws of
a world distinctly not our own. The qualities
of permanence and energy implicit in this
realm are extraordinary; although it welcomes
both men and animals into its system, it yields
nothing to them—it incorporates them. New
images are constantly being composed on the
same figures.

Henri Focillon[44]

Look hard at the configurations within the confines of great ornament (figures 7.1 and 7.2). Dismiss for a moment any thought of their
decorative function and concentrate exclusively on the way that elements such as posts, scrolls, lotuses, peonies, and clouds interconnect
to form dynamic compositions. Observe how the outstanding examples
of Egyptian, Greek, Roman, Gothic, Renaissance, and Victorian ornaments incorporate fragments such as heads, wings, and leafage (figure
7.3) that, in their original state, belong to complete and ordinary animals, birds, and plants. Isn't it curious that *inside* the limited space of
ornament, that is, within a frieze or band of foliation, wings on horses
or foliage growing out of heads can seem quite natural despite the fact
that were they to appear in the course of everyday life, such appearances would be regarded as unnatural, supernatural, or at least freak-
ish? What inspired the great cultures over the centuries to accept these
extraordinary hybrids as well as to celebrate their nonsense by placing
them in exalted locations atop important buildings and around the
edges of elegant bowls? Moreover, how did these metamorphoses come
into being in the first place?

In chapter 3, "The Linguistic Nature of Ornament," I pointed out
that ornament combines at least two levels of meaning. The most basic
level is the form of the utility inherent to the object of ornamentation,
while the other level brings actions, meanings, and figures that adhere
to the expressions of utility. This other level implicates life that origi-
nates in the world at large. Within the confines, that is, the limited

*7.2 All the elements within the
Chinese foliated scroll interconnect.
Xiangtangshan, Hebei province,
China, 6th century* A.D.

7.3 This Pompeian fresco incorporates fragments of originally "complete" beings.

space, of ornament, there are collisions, combinations, and mediations of elements innate to both the inherent and the adherent worlds. From the linguistic standpoint, such collisions, combinations, and mediations are fueled by the pendular and temporal drives of rhythm, in which events on either side of the axis of translation (figure 7.4) are drawn into the middle of a fantastic realm that is the heartland of ornament. Of course, such a realm cannot admit everything from without in whole cloth. In fact, if everything were to be admitted intact—such as the entire body of a bird rather than simply the wings or wing likenesses—there would be no mediation but instead a crowd of conflicted creatures. Ornament would be merely a depository or an anarchy of distinct beings. In this respect, the realm of ornament is not just a place of gathering but is also a place in which dismemberment and combination are sanctioned. In order to mediate among things, the mechanisms of ornament must divide, transform, and reconventionalize the articles of mediation as well as the meanings implicit in the states in which they were born. This peculiar activity creates *metamorphoses*, which obey the laws of ornament.

The British psychoanalyst Donald Winnicott identifies, in our coping with reality, the psychological function of what I am calling metamorphosis. Regarding the workings of metamorphosis as an important part of our healthy engagement with the world, he speaks of moments in our lives when certain external realities or appearances must be dissolved into fragments only to be reformed and differently combined into emerging and future realities. He describes such moments as transitional spaces or gaps that occur in the course of our normal mental and cultural lives. In the psychological sense, they are periods after which we can gradually modify our orientations to reality. As such, they are mental places of growth, renewal, and re-creation.

Winnicott regards our routine dependence on the ordinary environment, especially the social environment, as a necessary tyranny with which we must comply, and thus "human development [is] an often ruthless struggle against compliance with the environment."[45] A scientist of the mind, he analyzes the phenomenon of metamorphosis in regard to the crucial development of an infant. At first, there is an integration between the child and his or her original environment, which is the mother. As the child develops, a transitional space, or we might say a transitional duration, is established between the mother and the dependent child in which a critical unintegration is allowed for a period of time without the terror of disintegration. The child is establishing a personal identity while simultaneously identifying with the mother. The period of unintegration is coincident with the emergence of a consciousness about space itself, posited in the child's discovery of a personal inside world and an extrapersonal outside world. That emergence occurs in moments of playfulness and nonsense that are buttressed by the holding power, utility, and thus the context of the mother. These moments propose an "independence gained through acknowledgement of dependence,"[46] and so for Winnicott there is actually no such thing as independence but rather a dream of independence, which occurs while the child is still connected to the necessary supports, utilities, and authorities provided by a practical environment. Such a transitional space, treated here as the space of metamorphosis, is just as important as the practical supports that permit its existence. Within that space, the conflicting conditions that pervade life are admitted, rediscovered, and marshaled. The transitional spaces of metamorphosis continue to occur throughout our lives as we reexamine our dependencies. Mature adults bring vitality to that which is ancient, old, and orthodox by re-creating it after destroying it,[47] a re-creation that ultimately restores a measure of compliance with the environment.

We might characterize ordinary utilitarian objects, such as bowls and houses, as articles of dependency. We depend upon these necessities in order to live, and thus their objecthood and the space they provide belong to the practical realities of the surrounding world. We need such objects, but we also need our dreams and desires to be inde-

7.4 Events on either side of the axis of translation are drawn into a fantastic realm.

7.5 Eaves and entrances are sites where a building makes contact with the world outside itself. Louis Sullivan, Merchant's National Bank, Grinnell, Iowa, 1914.

7.6 A roof fence proclaims the border between the building and the sky. U.S., 19th century.

pendent of the constraints inherent to the world of reality those objects present. We need our houses, but we also wish to dwell in a larger world beyond the limits of houses. In the body of a house, the places of contact with the world beyond are transitional spaces such as the thresholds between roof and sky (figures 7.5 and 7.6) or between front door and street (figure 7.7). In a similar way, the thresholds or thick edges immediately between the body of any utilitarian object and the world beyond are transitional spaces. Ornament along such borders can exceed the efficacy of the utilitarian form and poetically question compliance with utility per se. Such thresholds and edges, treated as in-between spaces, are usually slender like the shoreline, marginal, and well suited to the ambivalence of ornament. They are also well suited to linear distribution of the repeating cycles of rhythmized foliation.

Metamorphosis is therefore twice expressed by ornament: first, in the figural mutation away from the utilitarian form of the object; and, second, in the extraordinary formation of metamorphoses within the internal space of ornament (figures 7.8 and 7.9). In both instances, the beings apprehended from either side of the space of ornament are momentarily dismembered and their fragments subjected to a lively and temporal state of combination.

In Western objects, the thickest edges are often outer or upper edges, such as the capitals atop columns or the fretwork along bor-

7.7 The threshold between the
front door and the street is also
a transitional space. Captain's
House, Stonington, Connecticut,
19th century.

ders of a rug. However, the area of expressiveness can also be compressed into a geographic center, such as an upward-pointing obelisk
in a plaza or a winged column on a bridge (figures 7.10 and 7.11).
Moments of transition are most obvious along an outer edge, where
the activity of the ornament proposes a mutation or an efflorescence.
Foliated and winged objects display and emblematize metamorphosis, and thus the Corinthian capital appears to be growing out of a
rigid support, while the fretwork around a carpet appears to emerge
from the margins of useful space. The basic expressions of utility,
whether structural or spatial, are thus disrupted and partially
opposed by the advent of figures from beyond the threshold as they
are apprehended and transformed into metamorphoses not in compliance with those governing our rational model of reality. Yet the

7.8 Mutation away from the
original utilitarian form of the
object: a hexafoil sprouts from
a luminaire at Yale University.

7.9 An example of the extraordinary
formation of metamorphoses within
the internal space of ornament.

7.10, 7.11 Winged piers situate the moment of metamorphoses into a center lace. Winged Bridge, Merritt Parkway, Connecticut, 20th century.

hybrids succeed in becoming identities in their own right, often to be named, perpetuated, and added, like the Greek palmette (figure 7.12), to the conventional vocabulary of visual language. Indeed, remarkably, conventionalized metamorphoses can remain intact for hundreds or thousands of years.

Unlike the vocabulary and grammar of rational language, the figures and line work of ornament do not attempt to denote or refer directly to anything usually found in scientific encyclopedias or in the halls, backyards, and woodlands of antiquity. But the nonsense of visual ornament does evoke, suggest, and allude to fragments of real shapes and activities that exist in the world, while occasionally permitting a fantastic creature to erupt out of the carnival of ornament's nar-

7.12 The Greek palmette was a hybrid that became a customary figure over time.

ration. As the special figures of ornament become our conscious and memorable property, they achieve a familiarity and metaphoric reality of their own. The unintegration and hybridization of evocative and fictional beings seem appropriate in the texture of visual rhythm. Thus ornament and some of its persistent elements, far more than being limited to a particular culture, a particular iconography, or a period of history, are most basically a level of human expression that evokes the existence of metamorphosis in our lives. A specific vocabulary may mark a particular context, such as the cloud and dragon in Chinese ornament, while the universality of ornament's language keeps on admitting, dismembering, and restructuring any number of contextual elements into the liminal space of objects.

GOTHIC METAMORPHOSIS

It will not do to say [ornaments] simply
[exist] in space: a work of art treats space
according to its own needs, defines space
and even creates such space as may be
necessary to it. . . . Even if reduced merely
to a slender and sinuous line, it is already
a frontier, a highway . . . [that] shapes,
straightens and stabilizes the bare and
arid field on which it is inscribed.

Henri Focillon[48]

For the sake of analysis, we might say that ornament is "linelike" and its objects are "formlike." Such descriptive terms approach the special way that ornament performs. By considering ornament a rhythmic system of linear figuration, we can envision its zigzags, spirals, and radiations as moving across the frozen terrain of architectural forms such as domes, walls, or cornices. Seen in this way, ornament is active and mobile, while its objects are rigid and stable. Of course, these descriptions belong to the realm of visual perception and the psychology of how we perceive and remember images. Because the figures of ornament are usually dynamic, they tend to be apprehended as temporal, gestural, and cyclic—mercurial in our minds. In contrast, the most basic forms of Euclidian geometry, like the circle and the square, become immediately fixed and memorable.

In this chapter, I consider the unique linear ornament found in Gothic architecture, particularly the development of its tracery during the seminal twelfth and thirteenth centuries, although new variations continued to appear into the twentieth century. Since Gothic tracery was created more recently than the great conventionalized ornaments of antiquity, its origins are far less mysterious. Analyzing these origins yields a glimpse into a design process in which two levels of meaning were combined into an entirely new species of ornament. Indeed, in its most dynamic form Gothic tracery is a splendid manifestation of metamorphosis rendered in modern geometry.

8.1 The facade of Rouen Cathedral. France, 13–15th century.

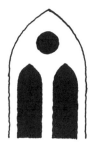

8.2 *The earliest form of Gothic tracery was a circle over two lancets.*

8.3 *The circle elaborated into a trefoil set above two lancets.*

8.4 *A further elaboration set a quatrefoil into a circular molding.*

8.5 *The early form of tracery is called plate tracery, because the shapes are cut into stone "plates."*

The following chronicle does not presume to be a rigorous art-historical account of the complex shifts in meanings given to the individual examples of tracery, and it barely mentions issues of iconography. I pay close attention to the precise figural moves taken over time by medieval artisans and the ways in which these moves constitute a species of gestural line work belonging to the basic grammar of visual language. Tracery was above all a visual—indeed, an architectural—accomplishment, in which certain critical features may be understood in their own graphic terms apart from their cultural context. Perhaps Gothic tracery is the best example of a nearly pure system of ornament that is partly rooted in earthly construction and partly involved in the imagining of a distant cosmos. Its emergence and ultimate flowering were an incremental process, an exploration in which the impulse to ornament found a receptive, plastic, and visually fluid medium in the linear shafts of carved stone (figure 8.1).

The Elements of Tracery

Most Gothic cathedrals were built entirely of stone up to the framing of the roof. The buildings descended from large Romanesque structures with massive walls capped with barrel vaults. The Romanesque walls were pierced with relatively small and undivided openings topped with semicircular arches. Such simple, even mundane, windows did not adequately express the Gothic vision, which sought to transcend the ordinary character of earthly windows by creating extraordinary openings in which the illumination of the heavens might be expressed.

The earliest signs of Gothic tracery were simply subordinate openings, such as a circle over two lancets inside the frame of the arch (figure 8.2). Like their forerunners the Romanesque windows, these openings were fashioned from stone walls with minimal framing elements. An elaboration of the scheme shaped the circle into a trefoil (figure 8.3). A further elaboration, in which a quatrefoil is surrounded with a circular molding, graced the pierced wall below with shafts and capitals (figure 8.4). The shafts, capitals, and archivolts express the idea of a miniature building with its two lower arches partially foiled. The line work articulating the foils and the windows runs along the borders of openings cut into the plane of the wall. The wall remains intact as a stone plate and, hence, this early form of tracery has been called *plate tracery* (as illustrated by the cutaway in figure 8.5).

Over time, the Gothic mason removed the plates or infilling

between the surrounding wall and the moldings to allow the structure to consist entirely of the interior moldings freestanding, so to say, inside the major arch (figure 8.6). This immediately increases the number of openings and begins to produce the silhouette of a linear configuration.

With this development of nearly free line work, the tracery becomes an entity in its own right, being the background of openings rather than being cut into a wall. In this new form, called *bar tracery*, the linear cusps of the quatrefoils and the trefoils within the lancets become figurally independent of the window frame. In the triforium of

8.6. *Tracery changed when the stone plate was virtually eliminated and freestanding interior molding formed the shapes.*

8.7 *In bar tracery the number of openings increased dramatically. Angel Choir, Lincoln Cathedral, mid-13th century.*

8.8 *Tracery performs as a system of line work in the interior window of Sainte-Chapelle, Paris.*

the Angel Choir at Lincoln Cathedral (figure 8.7), the number of openings within a single unit of arcade increases considerably, while the bars of the shafts and archivolts become sculptural elements emphasized by repetition. In the lofty window of Sainte-Chapelle (figure 8.8), a variation of this scheme includes three trefoils at the top. In this example, tracery can be identified as a figural system of bars of consistent thicknesses appearing as line work beneath the powerful boundary of a great arch. The mutations of this line work over time in the great endwall windows of the High Gothic cathedrals tell a story of ornament in the making.

GREAT WINDOWS

The lower interior body of the cathedral was intended to be a manifestation of the ideal celestial city. The vestibule to that city lay behind the cathedral's west facade, an enormous work of architectural design acting, as Von Simpson puts it, "as a threshold leading from the life in this world to the eternity that lies beyond it."[49] The walk through the front door into the body of the cathedral was to be an epiphany, a moment of virtual transition from this world to the other. Such a work articulated the connection between the "here," manifested in a divine image of an earthly city, and the "there," a vision of the cosmos impressed into the upper reaches of the architecture. From a design standpoint, this was an extraordinary juxtaposition. Whereas cities were human artifacts subject to the laws of gravity and deploying common elements of building such as columns, arches, and roofs, the cosmos was understood by monastic scholars as being manifest in an ideal geometry of pure ratios independent of gravity. The cosmos was thought to transcend the mundane laws of construction. How then could the line work belonging to a unified work of architecture combine these two distinct worlds?

The tracery within the great Gothic rose windows, in which elegant metamorphoses are vividly expressed in struggling and delicate line work, provides answers. The transitional space situated within the great windows became the chosen home of ornament, itself the meeting point of two worlds.

In Abbot Suger's very early Gothic facade at the Abbey of St.-Denis (figure 8.9), a circular opening is cut out of the stone wall and flanked by slender blind portals. The circular "rose" is positioned directly above

8.9 In the early Gothic facade of St.-Denis a circular opening is cut from the stone wall. Mid-12th century.

8.10 The western facade of Chartres Cathedral refines the model of St.-Denis by enlarging the rose window above a three-arch opening. Early 13th century.

the entrance and is flanked by two blind windows. The lower three portals begin to form an arcade. This scheme is refined at Chartres' western facade (figure 8.10), where an enlarged rose window begins to impinge upon the top of a three-part arcade below. Immediately above the arcade, vertical pilasters and the horizontal moldings situate the rose within a square wall segment. Within the plate tracery of the rose window, a ring of twelve octafoils is connected to a central dodecafoil, with twelve spokes or columns that seem like spinning classical orders. In many twelfth-century rose windows, the spectacle of the ancient orders in free spin suggests the special defiance of gravity allowed to ornament, especially an ornament constituted to present the idea of the transcendent cosmos.

Consider that the upper portion of the composition, in which the rose is situated, belongs to the realm of the cosmos, while the lower part, or the arcade with its row of conventional vertical supports, represents the celestial city. If the purpose of the ornament is to mediate between these two realms, its line work must be concentrated between the circling elements of the upper portion and the repetitive vertical elements of the lower arcade (figure 8.11). Within the transitional space of ornament, new figures must be designed that accept the visual evocations of both the cosmos and the city.

In the west facade of Laon (figure 8.12), the rose grows to the full width of its subordinate arcade, which includes five bays. Thus the cosmic rose and its subordinate arcade are beginning to be unified within the dimensions of an all-encompassing arch. At Laon, the rose window and the openings along the arcade are still cut out of the wall in the early Gothic manner. Although the two outermost registers of the semicircular and circular openings are transforming in the direction of bar tracery, the innermost dodecafoil with its greater mass employs the earlier plate tracery.

The rose window of Chartres' north transept employs similar half-circular shapes around the perimeter, whereas the center has a much smaller dodecafoil, from which the tracery moves outward through twelve shafts to a ring of twelve squares and thence to a ring of quatrefoils terminated by a ring of twelve half-circles (figure 8.13). The immense circular framing element surrounding the forty-nine interior subdivisions is carved in the dimensions and manner of bar tracery and is virtually identical in shape to the mullions tracing the geometry throughout the interior of the window. In this scheme, all the "freestanding" elements within the great arch tend to appear similar in weight and thus to belong to a uniform species of line work. Small lin-

8.11 The circling lines of the rose window and the vertical lines of the arcade.

8.12 At Laon the linear and circular elements are reconciled by expanding the window to the width of the arcade.

8.13 Small intermediate shafts unify the rose window at Chartres.

97

8.14 The radiation of the tracery from the center of the rose window is more confidently expressed than at Chartres. St.-Denis, north transept.

8.15 The divisive horizontal line beneath the rose is awkwardly eliminated as the arcade pushes upward. Tours Cathedral, early 14th century.

ear elements uphold the underside of the rose from the ridge immediately above the lower arcade. From that horizontal ridge, or ledge, to the great semicircular arch above, a system of regularized line work has come into existence that draws attention to itself as a delicate composition. During this same period, emphasis shifts from the contained, static sensibility of Chartres' west window to the radiating, outward-pushing sensibility of its north window. The entire north composition proposes an outward expansion.

In the north transept of St.-Denis (figure 8.14), radiation is more confidently expressed. It starts at the center with a hexafoil, proceeds outward through two layers of radiating spokes, and resolves into twenty-four hexafoils about the outer edge. The rhythmic pulse of the subordinate arcade also increases to an A-B-A-B-A-B pattern producing ten major bays and twenty minor lancets, in comparison to the A-A-A-A-A-A pattern of regular supports in the north transept of Chartres. The divisive horizontal ledge still prevents a fluid connection between the cosmos above and the arcaded representation of a celestial city immediately below.

That sharp horizontal division is eliminated in the somewhat awkward resolution of the transition between rose and arcade at Tours (figure 8.15). The shaping of the tracery, its bar moldings, trefoils, and quatrefoils, is almost identical above and below the lower half of the bulging square frame enclosing the rose. The geometric shapes along the border between the celestial city and the cosmos are merging into a single species.

Across the channel, the English architects and stonemasons appear to have been less conservative or committed to the rigidity of the seminal examples of great windows. They favored a livelier set of shapes and a more complicated arrangement of connections between the outer rim of the rose and the arches topping off the lower arcade. This resulted in a loosening up and an enlargement of the element of tracery occupying the transitional zone between above and below. For example, in Ripon Minster (figure 8.16), two large pointed arches press up underneath on either side of the rose with framing that runs tangentially into the large circular molding. This juxtaposition produces a major polyplike shape pushing upward and outward from the two thick central shafts of the arcade. The same two shafts also curve inward to produce a slender pointed arch that penetrates into the base of the rose. The four remaining posts are comparatively slender and uphold clusters of cinquefoils harboring delicate circles.

Within the west window of Exeter Cathedral (figure 8.17), the two major and central minor arches, reminiscent of Ripon's arcade, occupy a much greater portion of the window's opening than does the diminutive row of shafts along the arcade. Thus within the great arch of the window the majority of space is dedicated to transitional figuration. Widths are greatly regular throughout the composition, and a certain geometric rigor is evident in the large set of regular polygons. All manner of trefoils, quatrefoils, and cinquefoils are rigidly fixed throughout the window. Perhaps the most remarkable apparition is the five-pointed star in the eye of the rose with its outer row of points shaped like foiled Gothic arches. The geometric similarity of the foils in the stars and the foils in the arcade establish symmetric relations between the elements of rotation belonging to the physics of the cosmos above with the gravity-bound arches belonging to the Earth below. Yet despite the relatively large amount of tracery above a diminished arcade, the great circle remains the most important figure at Exeter.

In the east window of Selby Abbey (figure 8.18), there is a greater elasticity and organic continuity between the openings in the tracery as they become asymmetric and distended. The diminished "rose" has become almond-shaped and double-centered. The bars of tracery

8.16 In Ripon Minster the central lancet penetrates the rose.

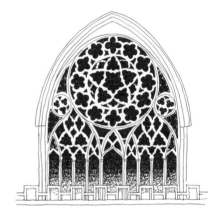

8.17 The line work between arcade and rose becomes more continuous and elastic at Exeter Cathedral.

8.18 Greater elasticity and continuity is developed within the line work of Selby Abbey.

8.19 Within the east window of Carlisle Cathedral virtually every other shape is either distended or squeezed. England, mid-14th century.

8.20 The heart at the center of the great window was an alternate vision of the cosmic realm. York Cathedral, England, early 15th century.

8.21 If the heart of the York window produced a tree, the window of the Prague Cathedral produced a headdress at the center.

have become more branchlike, thorny, and turbulent, while the spaces created by the tracery are less polygonal and more leaflike. There is a particularly abrupt transition between the curvilinear tracery above and the slender rhythmic row of columns below. Within this English excursus, all of the transitional space has moved upward from the middle to occupy the realm formerly reserved for the circular rotating cosmos.

The east window of Carlisle Cathedral (figure 8.19) combines regular symmetrical quatrefoils with stretched or distended quatrefoils. Three regular quatrefoils are prominently located in the elliptical core of the space originally occupied by the rose higher up inside it. Two more quatrefoils are situated in the compressed triangles on either side of the ellipse. Virtually every other opening is distended or squeezed. Of particular interest are the two sets of leaf shapes within leaf shapes to the right and left, their lower cusps springing from five-legged joints that issue from large vertical stems in the arcade. It is difficult to believe the builders did not have trees and plants in their thoughts, although on occasion leaves, trees, and tracery may obey similar laws of structure. Certainly, the English seemed bent on extinguishing the traces of regular classical geometry that emblematized the seminal expression of cosmos.

A beautiful moment of metamorphosis in the history of the great window occurred when an upward-sprouting, heart-shaped apparition appeared in the center at York Cathedral (figure 8.20). It is particularly significant that this new figure, commanding the space of the sanctuary, manages to rival the Platonic geometry of the great roses that had dominated the seminal French windows for more than a hundred years. It is an alternate vision of the cosmic realm, a vision more akin to earthly nature and the art of the builder than to the contemplative art of geometric speculation practiced in a monastery with a compass and a sheet of paper. But it is no less a metaphor of the universe, and in some ways it solves the problem of connecting the idea of the cosmos with the ordinary elements of a manufactured city below in an organic expression moving to incorporate the arboreal figures of terrestrial nature. It is an architectural gift born in the cauldron of metamorphosis. Indeed, the heart shape growing out of the central climax of the rhythmic arcade below is the epitome of a metamorphosis.

Another surprising metamorphosis occurs in the west window of the cathedral in Prague (figure 8.21). This accomplishment, actually not completed until the early twentieth century, required a special type of tracery in which its bars appear to weave through one another. This allows another set of geometric figures to appear out of the line work.

Great half-circles weave through subordinate line work to span eight units of a twelve-unit arcade to produce two huge intersecting lower arches. The arcade below is a rhythmic sequence of single-double-single-double shafts surmounted with a composition of small to bigger arches that issue a galaxy of trefoils, quatrefoils, cinquefoils, and twelve- and sixteen-cusped polygons. Most extraordinary, however, is the eruption of the immense crown of King Wenceslas in the climactic almond-shaped element beneath the summit of the entire arrangement. If York produced a tree, Prague produced a headdress in the eye of a mandorla.

At this point the story turns back to France, where it all got started. The rose window of the south transept of Amiens, erected in the early sixteenth century, seems to incorporate every figural move thus far and still conserve the seminal idea of a great circle over an urbane arcade (figure 8.22). Line work controls the entire composition, from the five pediments supported by a row of twenty blind arches to the arcade with A-B-A-B-A-pattern shafts housing sixteen windows reaching up to touch the rim of the twenty-four-pointed rose. The earlier English leaflike line work has been delivered to the radiant and flamboyant rose, along with an interweave of major and minor thicknesses of branchlike bar tracery moving over and underneath one another. Evidently, the master of Amiens was not ready to jettison the original horizontal line between the bottom of the rose and the top of the arcade; but he did limit its thickness to the standard of tracery and extended the shafts of the lower arcade upward through the bar to produce a second set of pointed arches above six of the eight lancets.

Although the turbulent traceries of York, Prague, and Amiens were descended from the particular allegory of connecting the celestial city with the cosmos, they provide an important lesson about the nature of ornament beyond its function to express a particular mythology prescribed by its culture. They reveal the way that the line work within ornament demands and creates its own space and, indeed, creates such shapes as may be necessary to resolve and express the struggle to combine different types of geometry and different levels of meaning. It is not enough to propose that the great figures of York and Prague respond only to their seminal iconography, as they appear to issue as well from the unpredictable and creative power of the rhythm pulsing within the transitional space of enormous windows. These metamorphoses must be understood as inventions not unlike the spontaneous phrases we find in musical improvisation emerging from the intersecting elements of meter and sound. Such an understanding locates within ornament a unique world of figuration drawn from the rhythmized

8.22 The great window of Amiens Cathedral incorporates every figural move in the Gothic tradition while still preserving the original form—a circle set above a horizontal bar. France, 16th century.

combinations of many things. Yet by comparing York, Prague, and Amiens we can also detect the capacity for those traceries to inscribe an imprint of the particular ethos belonging to their respective communities and moments in history.

THE LIMITS OF GOTHIC'S LINEAR ORNAMENT

The proposal made at the beginning of this chapter that ornament is always linelike and its objects formlike will have to be modified, because line work in the form of shafts, ribs, moldings, and tracery exists throughout the Gothic interior and is not limited to its tracery. How then might we characterize the line work belonging to the most basic language of architecture compared to that which belongs to the language of architectural ornament? It is difficult to put an exact edge on the limits of Gothic ornament, because the Gothic line work throughout the entire sanctuary, that is, the principal interior space, is so dominant and evocative. However, we can discern a boundary if we adhere to the notion that metamorphoses are critical properties of ornament.

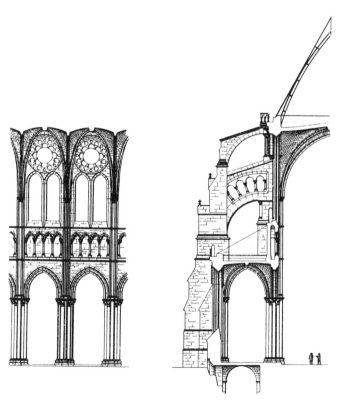

8.23 The delicate stack of interior arcades and windows is supported from without by massive buttresses. Chartres Cathedral.

Like the line work of tracery, the linear shafts and ribs of High Gothic interiors are not necessary from the standpoint of the building's basic structure, nor do they truly denote the system by which the edifice is fundamentally supported. The entire building is a massive structure that surrounds multistoried arcades and window walls rising from the great pillared arcades along the floor of the nave. The stack of interior arcades and window walls are stiffened from without by buttresses springing from enormous heaps of stone (figure 8.23). These stabilizing heaps are the greatest single elements of mass, and they are positioned outside the building and are visible only from the exterior. Inside, given the pillared sanctuary wall as a load-bearing structure in its own right, the delicate networks of shafting that run over the surface of the arcades from the floor to the vaulting above are largely redundant from the standpoint of structural economy. Their physical work, if they do any, could be absorbed into a single pier running from floor to ceiling or by the thick sanctuary wall with openings. In other words, the apparently structural line work upon the interior nave wall (figure 8.24) and vaults is there to express something beyond structure. Indeed, the interior layer of shafting evokes a fantastic image of construction that aspires to articulate a heavenly rather than an earthly edifice. Is it not reasonable, therefore, to include such a fantasy, rooted in the vision of a transcendent world, as a property of ornament?

At first, the answer seems to be yes. Why shouldn't we include fantastic expressions of construction as appropriate subject matter for architectural ornament, which mediates between the ordinary and the extraordinary? This response seems perfectly reasonable until we consider the nature of *spatial utility* rather than *constructional utility*. One of the responsibilities of architecture is to provide ample space for particular activities and ceremonies. Indeed, the primary activity of the cathedral is to marshal a large congregation into a magnificent place in order that the human and the superhuman, the mortal and the immortal may be assembled and accommodated. Inside the enormous structure, the congregation is ceremoniously welcomed and subordinate spaces are provided for a pantheon of souls as they gather to celebrate that event.

The congregation assembles on the ground level, the clergy might visit the tribunes on the second level, and above are higher and greater levels for the immortals. Within hundreds of interior and exterior niches are small, medium, and large places provided for members of the sacred society. Each of these collective and singular spaces is enshrined and articulated with seemingly identical types of slender vertical shafts and archivolts, all belonging to a regular species of architectural line work distributed at multiple scales throughout the cathedral. This uniformity of ideal Gothic detail is noted by Erwin Panofsky as an "arrangement according to a system of homologous parts and parts of parts."[50] Compositions of similar shafts range in size from several feet for smaller beings to nearly a hundred feet for greater beings, and, from these shafts, pointed arches spring in a hierarchy of sizes and shapes consisting of scores of delicately pointed pavilions nested together. Spaces ranging from the miniature to the magnificent culminate in the splendid apex of the crossing of aisles, which centers the entire interior space.

Returning to the question of whether the preponderance of line work in the sanctuary is a property of ornament or of architecture's most basic language, we now can point to the latter. Most of the line work, while seeming to be fantastic construction, actually defines realms of space meant to be occupied by mortals or immortals. The architecture organizes those spaces of occupation through respective dimensions that correspond directly to the ascension of ranks within the multitude. Indeed, no task is more central to architecture than to provide housing, be it for mortals or immortals, as it simultaneously expresses the idea of housing.

Gothic's seminal ornament flourishes within the transitional spaces of tracery. There, expressions of utility are partially dissolved as they become involved with another realm beyond the construction and beyond the spatial hierarchies of housing. This realm was expected to display a brilliance capable of further dissolving the edifice and denying its bondage to gravity. We must grant that the rose window and the quatrefoil pay scant attention to terrestrial law as their line work revolves around its own center point; yet if that rotating function did not itself reach downward and convene architecturally with the shafts reaching upward from the city, the rose—as in our first example, at St.-Denis—would be an autonomous display of heavenly geometry functioning as a decoratively placed symbol. There would be no manifestation of the metamorphic event. However, when the line work emanating from the rose and the line work rising from the arcades below are absorbed into special zones of transition, a new space is created and a new form of ornament emerges (figure 8.25). The outer boundaries of that new space, the frames of traceried metamorphoses, define the limits of Gothic's linear ornament.

8.24 The apparently structural line work upon the interior walls of Laon evokes a fantastic and heavenly edifice.

9.1 A painting of the Turtle Dance
performed in Taos Puebla.

THE RHYTHMIZED BODY
IN ARCHITECTURE

> The [dancing] chorus . . . is a dancistic mass.
> Its movements are not the expression of what
> it is feeling individually. It moves according
> to impersonal laws. It might be compared
> to some work of architecture come to life,
> moving, transforming itself from one shape
> to another.
>
> *Arthur Michel*[51]

Early in the morning on New Year's Day, 1987, I watched the Turtle Dance performed by the natives in the large open, rectangular plaza constituting the town center of Taos Puebla in New Mexico. Dancers assembled in a linear formation (figure 9.1), a "chorus line," positioning themselves to face inward along the west side of the space, between the dead center and the row of buildings to the west. For a few moments, I witnessed somewhat indirectly what I have come to understand academically as the visual nature of ornament in the fabric of architecture. The dancing included the pounding of feet accompanied by chanting and the gestural raising and lowering of implements. At one moment, every dancer revolved to face the row of dwellings and then completed the revolution to again face the center. Their revolutions were like scrolls. After completing the dance, the chorus walked over to the northern side, reformed, and repeated their movements. They moved once again, to the south side. I have never seen a more potent expression of place: the practical assembly of dwellings along the edge was exalted by the figuration of dance. The sanctity of the soil underneath was proclaimed by the stomping feet as the absolute location of the place was affirmed by the visual attention paid by the chorus to the center of the Puebla. Their bodies in concert reiterated the square form of the plaza.

This experience confirmed my suspicion that dance is a basic form of communication that allows an amount of understanding across cultural lines. Although I did not know the very specific meanings or the visual notations belonging to the dancers' belief, I comprehended some meaning through the power of the spectacle. Such visual comprehension occurred on the spot, and I will never forget it.

It was also an occasion to witness the combining of temporally ordered dancing figures with a spatially ordered community of buildings. Gathered in the center of the public square, we viewed the unadorned adobe dwellings through a layer of rhythm. The space of the dance was a threshold from which the dancers looked both inside and outside their line of translation. If their outward attention had been toward only the prairie or the night, the performance might have been about bleakness; yet those buildings, by their provision of shelter, gave place and meaning to the dance. At the same time, the dance articulated a dream of the culture absent in the utilitarian facts of building. The buildings seemed to accept the dance as a fulfillment of what they lacked in specific expression, and thus the dance completed the Puebla's identity as a settlement with history, vision, and authority.

Our most basic understanding of three-dimensional form is first realized by the experience of our own bodies dwelling, standing, and moving. It is through our bodies, our corporeality, that we first come to comprehend, organize, and give meaning to external things. By directly engaging objects, we begin to distinguish the formations and complexity of their details. With aggressive and defensive movements, the living body discovers the space between persons and objects.

We come to recognize the separateness of external objects after we unconsciously locate our bodies inside a three-dimensional boundary (figure 9.2). This psychological threshold is positioned beyond the body and demarcates "inside" personal space from "outside" extrapersonal space. As an unstable boundary subject to events impinging from either side, it may be regarded as a psychological property of the physical body's possessed and manageable territory. Because it is vital and elastic, we may characterize it as a layer with thickness or, better, with variations of thickness (figure 9.3), opacity and transparency positioned between a person's sense of the internal and external worlds on either side. In this respect, it is more than just space; it is an active place, or we might say a type of transitional space in which impulses gathered from both sides are admitted into a struggle. The ancient Ionians spoke of such a space-place as a chora, "a scant space between, such as that between a horse and a chariot, . . . or the narrow rim of shoreline left for the Achaeans to fight in."[52]

The second most fundamental principle governing our comprehension of three-dimensional form is found in each person's sense of

9.2 We locate our personal space within a three-dimensional boundary.

9.3 Personal boundaries vary in distance under different circumstances.

an interior world (figure 9.4), a heartland with a center. A person does not imagine his or her personal space to be hollow but rather to be full of important, organized feelings of *up/down, front/back, right/left,* and *here* in the center. The *right/left* coordinate, which psychologically includes the entire body, always remains at right angles to the frontal orientation of the face, despite any contortions or oblique movements of the body in relation to the face. Forward motion signifies strength and virtue, whereas backward motion has private, unsafe, and weak implications. As I have written elsewhere, "We tell people to back down when they have gone too far forward, but when they have a purposeful goal like parking a car we say back up."[53]

The face can perform as a facade (figure 9.5), acting as an important message system representing the rest of the body. Its gestures are metaphors of the body's experience. The face as facade sends messages about past experiences, present states, and future desires. In this respect, facial gestures substitute for body gestures and take on some of the characteristics of a second, rather more two-dimensional and schematized place of expression. Thus body meanings associated with *up/down, front/back,* and *here* in the center are articulated with smiles, frowns, and grimaces. Perhaps the most powerful expressions are signaled by the eyes, which in body-image literature are identified as having taking-in and incorporative-like significance. Altogether our capacity to express the hardening and softening of body boundaries, the extension and contraction of body orientations, and the importance of

9.4 We sense a world inside our bodies.

9.5 Our facial gestures can be a substitute for bodily gestures, acting as a metaphor of the body's experience.

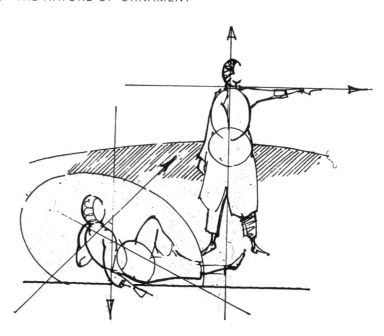

*9.6 The body's most basic orientation
is earthbound along the up/down axis.*

internal landmarks establishes a natural empathetic taxonomy of meanings belonging to visual language.

The basic orientation of *up/down* (figure 9.6) is guided by gravity, and no matter how the body moves, leans, and spins, its direction is earthbound. Verticality may be the most splendid provider of meaning, originating as a promising dimension from the struggle to stand up, walk, and grow. Upward, which in the mobile body means upward from the waist, "indicates striving, fantasy, and aloofness, while downward, particularly in Western culture, is often depressing."[54] But we are also told to keep our feet on the ground and be realistic. Perhaps for the dancers at Taos as they stomp, down is a particularly exalted direction. Cultural differences confirm rather than confuse the importance of verticality as a provider of meaning. In Western culture there is an ambivalence, which tends to depend on whether we are addressing the ordinary or the extraordinary.

Within the Turtle Dance, complex meanings are expressed by the rhythmic movements and gestures, the holding of symbolic equipment, the chorus line of bodies juxtaposed with the rows of practical buildings. In the context of the Puebla, these elements display the particular vocabulary of the Taos people. But can such ceremonial ideas, rhythmized by the dance, find their way *directly* into the fabric of buildings? Can meanings originally derived from the movements of the human body become the visual property of rigid architectural elements? Can that dynamism be impressed within the expressive ele-

110

ments of construction, which must also obey the facts and economics of physics?

Spatial conditions associated with the body such as *inside/outside*, *front/back*, or *here* in the center, and haptic feelings, wrought from the sense of touch, such as *push-away/pull-in*, can be incorporated into architectural form with derivative and correspondent meanings. When the formal and material elements of building are organized to represent body boundaries, body orientations, and bodily actions in a mimetic or analogous manner, certain natural expressions may be communicated by the forms and line work of the architecture. Moreover, in addition to perceiving corporeal expressions in the external forms of objects such as buildings, we can enter these objects psychologically rather than entering them actually, by imagining the presence of bodylike boundaries that determine a separate object's inside and outside space. For example, we can imagine walking through and settling in the space of a miniature dollhouse and further imagine being inside a room in the dollhouse and looking out a window.

Although our empathetic capacity to imaginatively depart from personal space as though departing from a bubble, passing through a void, and entering another bubble of space is intuitively obvious, it defies any form of mathematical modeling. It is an accomplishment dependent on the haptic sense that each of us possesses a separate world constituted by his or her actual and psychological body and the corollary sense that other bodies and other things occupy separate worlds as well.

Thus, via the human perception of very basic corporeal meanings articulated in the elements, space, and details of architecture, architecture possesses a capacity to communicate a repertoire of affective meanings. In a mimetic way, buildings can be given and can give back a vocabulary of basic human feelings. But can that basic vocabulary be further developed to express less personal notions than, for example, "come in," "stay away," "I am jubilant," or "I am sad"? Can it express actions and formations that originate in other types of animal or botanical bodies, or in natural and mathematical systems altogether distinct from the human body?

In the language of ancient Western architecture, the connection between the expressions inherent to our bodies and the articulation of construction was brilliantly achieved. Embedded in the proportions and shape of the Greek column is the combined image of the human body and the upright post, or we might say the combination of empathetic form with utilitarian form (figure 9.7).

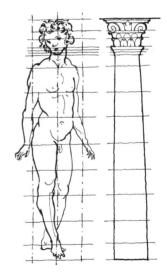

9.7 The proportions of the Greek column combine both utilitarian and empathetic form.

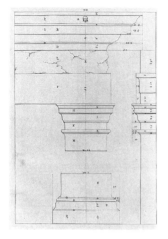

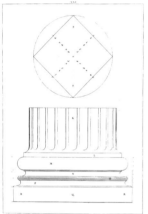

9.8 The Greek order contained residual features of the economic wooden post.

Part of the order's form necessarily derives from the economic structural shape of a post made to sit on a foundation and hold up a beam and the roof above. That part expresses the practical shape essential to the construction of a wooden hut or post-and-beam structure. However, by fleshing out key elements, making them bigger, and subdividing them into shapely and "geometrized" parts, the Greeks developed a new, artificial column containing only certain vestigial features of the original, economical post (figure 9.8). In mass and detail, the "ordered" column is an artifice, an invention that pays a kind of ceremonial attention to the crude facts of the economical post as it proceeds to establish an *idea* about that post and therefore an idea about the act of supporting per se. By becoming articulated as a very specific set of measured parts, the ancient order achieved a conventional identity. It became a visual "word" capable of reiterating its idea about "supporting" in any number of locations, sizes, and contexts. Its identity became fixed and framed with moldings to constitute, in John Summerson's words, the "bare elements of what is required to make the column a grammatical form of communication."[55]

Once the column was conventionalized, it could be distributed throughout the architecture to participate in the phrases and sentences of the greater vocabulary of architectural elements that constituted an entire building (figure 9.9). It remained a conspicuous figure belonging to a less conspicuous chorus of figures. By extending the

9.9 Conventionalized columns appear as conspicuous figures upon a facade. Venice, 16th-century translation of Vitruvius.

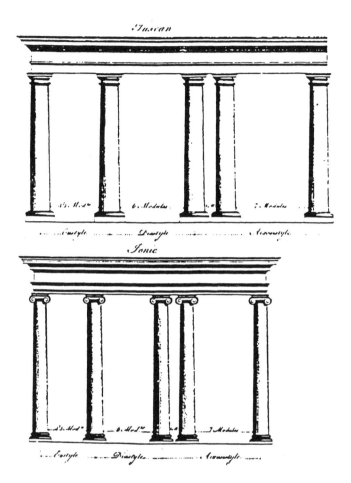

9.10 Rows of columns present both meter and rhythm.

length of a colonnade, a number of columns could be placed in line and their repetition subjected to a more rhythmic pattern. In rows of Tuscan, Doric, Ionic, and Corinthian columns, we can identify distinct meters and basic rhythms (figure 9.10). Alexander Tzonis and Liane Lefaivre refer to the spaces between the columns as "voids," with the columns being "stressed" (strong) and the voids being "unstressed" (weak). They acoustically describe the effect of serial solid-and-void patterns by presenting a sequence with one solid width to three void widths as sounding like "knock, tot, tot, tot, knock, tot, tot, tot."[56] Here Tzonis and Lefaivre recognize an important principle of spatial perception that declares solid objects, even when the spaces between them are shapely and larger in volume, to be visually more dominant and obtrusive than the voids. Thus solids almost always appear first in an unfolding of percepts.

However, the shaft and capital of the Greek order not only represent an idea about structural support, they also allude to the shape and

9.11 The human body enslaved within the form of a column.

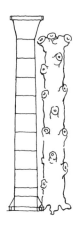

9.12 Columns imagined as tree trunks.

proportions of the human body. The art historian George Hersey has focused on the notion of a concealed human figure embodied within the outline of the order, and he has particularly characterized that occult body as a prisoner in bondage and as a person helping to hold up the building. He reports on the Renaissance painter Francesco di Giorgio's image of the origin of the Corinthian order embodying an enslaved woman (figure 9.11) as well as di Giorgio's depiction of the column as a tree trunk (figure 9.12). Seen either as a human body or a tree trunk, the column elicits our empathetic response, our sensing of forces within external things. We imagine the column as ourselves standing erect and, under stress, holding something up; we viscerally associate with the tree as though it were a kindred spirit.

From an architectural standpoint, the corporeal meanings given to the column do not displace its primary import, which is an idea about support. However, once we switch our perception from a mechanical to a human instrument of support, that is, from the impression of a cylindrical post to the feeling of an upright body, we can tell a far greater number of stories that convey the fundamental idea of support or that contain supporting elements. In the various stories involving this column, "support" may belong to the elements of a stone construction or may belong to the constituents of a social and political order or may be identified as the real or allegorical branches of a tree supporting an immense canopy.

In Greek architecture, the powerful colonnades on the ground level may be regarded as preparations for a sort of metalanguage that occurs above, yet in consonance with, the fundamental orders of architecture. The rows of heavy vertical piers, those stomps on the earth,

9.13 In the facade of the Parthenon, the columns set the meter for the rhythmized elements upon the entablature and cornice.

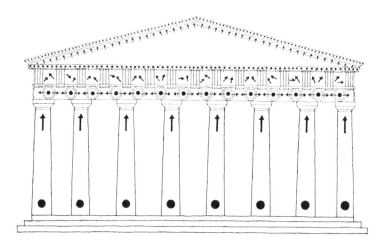

9.14 The centaurs in the frieze of the Parthenon have mobile orientations, enlivening the basic meter of the columns.

establish the basic meter for the rhythmized voices above as though they were the drums and bass notes of an orchestra.

The eight columns on the elevation of the Parthenon, for example, provide the basic meter, which is immediately doubled along the frieze by the triglyphs and metopes (figure 9.13). Each triglyph breaks down into three bars terminated below by a row of six guttae. The meter of the flat blocks containing the guttae, which are reflected above on the soffit, increases to thirty beats if regularly measured along the entire length of the entablature. The foliated scroll along the horizontal cornice has seventy-four cycles, while the raking cornice along the edge of the roof has almost one hundred.

As these subordinate elements increase in number and diminish in size, a new attitude of figuration moves away from the basic meter. Within the serial spaces of each metope, rearing centaurs (figure 9.14) dance along a zigzag horizontal path as fighting, falling, and fallen warriors engage in combat. Here a truly rhythmic passage of figures enlivens the regular pattern established below. The centaurs within the metopes present mobile orientations, their bodies gesturing and rotating in a greater number of directions. The upright stance of the Doric orders is superseded as the emerging figuration becomes a literal representation of humans and horses performing actions apart from the physical laws innate to construction and support. At this level of architectural expression, a more dynamic and gesturing chorus line evokes an animated and turbulent world of cycles and mutations. The increased number of movements and symmetries allow right- and left-handedness, rotation, and multiple responses to gravity. The fractal-like orchestration of proportions and symmetries provides a spectacle of mathematical organization.

The metamorphic nature of figures within the metopes reveals something else of critical importance. The centaur, a horse turning into a human figure, or vice versa, is a combinational figure in which the potency of two animals combines into an entity outside the taxonomy of earthly life. Such a metamorphosis emblematizes the transformation of one thing into another and thus evokes the idea that ordinary laws governing the architecture have been suspended. The utilitarian objects of everyday reality are dismembered and rearranged into imaginary forms. Extraordinary things are produced out of ordinary things.

In addition to providing mythic content, the centaurs and warriors, as additional kinds of bodies, superadd rhythm to the beat of the "human" bodies below, even as they remain coordinated with the basic meter of the basic architectural supports. These exotic creatures, apprehended from a historic mythology, mediate between the geometry of the colonnade below and the more turbulent foliated scrollwork impressed into the higher levels of the elevation.

Upon the cornice of the entablature, directly above the triglyphs and metopes, is a rhythmized band of foliation. It produces a pulsation of radiant lotuses, spirals, and waves in a medley of symmetries that remain in visual touch with the basic meter below. Within the scrollwork are the evocative cycles of botanical nature. A larger visual vocabulary has been born in the chosen home of metamorphoses, the etymology and persistence of which is fueled by a form of visual chanting (see chapter 7). Within the motility of the chant, the linguistic and mathematical workings of the mind are expressed. Perhaps the connection of the scrolls to the columns below represents a union of rhythmized thoughts and rhythmized meaningful elements of the body. The workings of the brain and the body are connected through rhythm.

Viewing the foliated scroll and its supportive colonnade together, we could say that the pulsating ornament above is marshaling the building from the head down, while the final expression of that ornament is a sequence of downbeats upon the platform below. Thus in one respect the basic chorus line prepares us for an ascent into an upper world of symmetries defiant of gravity, and simultaneously the cerebral antics of the ornament descend to exalt the ground. Seen in this way, ornament presides over the massive weight of the edifice. There is not only a movement upward into a more abstract, turbulent, and perhaps dematerialized chorus of voices in which ornament privileges a distancing from the earth, but also the reverse. We can recognize the finality of a particular place thanks to architectural footwork, particularly as we stand magnificently emplaced beside the great classical supports of architecture. From that vantage point, we cannot escape the tribute paid to the earth underneath by the ornament above.

The simultaneous presence of the virtual energy of the body and the apparent forces of construction so elegantly expressed in the language of ancient Greek architecture can readily be found in Gothic architecture as well. John Summerson characterized the Gothic as a "pile of heavenly mansions," the mansions being "aedicules," or architectural representations of small buildings, houses, or shrines that can be articulated in a wide range of sizes and distributed in rows or stacked vertically to construct a larger edifice.[57]

An individual aedicule is a two-posted shrine in a wall (figure 9.15) or a four-posted structure with a canopy (figure 9.16) serving as a house for a single human figure. The enshrined figure may be actual or imagined, but it always appears to occupy the space beneath the canopy. Usually it denotes a particular person belonging to the terrestrial or celestial elect. Unlike the solid columns of the Greek orders, in which an image of the human body is immersed, the aedicule immediately surrounds the space of the body and extends its psychological space to the limits of the aedicule's architectural elements. It marks the geometry of *front/back, left/right, up/down,* and *center.* The canopy evokes and exalts the upward direction of the head; the sill or pedestal is the foundation upon which the enshrined figure stands or sits.

In Gothic architecture, the statues or figures within aedicules or within panels of stained glass are almost always standing, gesturing, and actively looking at or holding something (figure 9.17). Specific per-

9.15 A two-posted aedicule houses a human image and architecturally extends the physiological boundary of that body.

9.16 In both the two-posted and the four-posted aedicule the presence of the human body can be either real or imagined.

9.17 In the Gothic aedicule, the enshrined figures are often dynamic, almost always standing, gesturing, and actively looking out.

117

sons, and thus specific ideas represented by each person, are placed in key locations within the pile of heavenly mansions according to the person's status and fate. Thus the aedicule is a conventionalized unit of space capable of simultaneously representing a small building and the real or occult presence of a body or bodies within the building. In concert, the aedicules may represent the affective ordering of an entire society.

The classic Gothic method was to build massive stone piers and buttresses first rising upward and finally turning inward to a culmination. Within these feats of engineering, medieval architects added aedicules held delicately erect upon ordered clusters of slender vertical shafts, the tallest of which connected to ribs located upon the vaulted ceilings of the enormous sanctuary (figure 9.18). The shafts and ribs acted in unison to form a geometric network of lines transcending the weight of the massive piers to which they were attached. The Gothic achievement was to superimpose an expressive layer of architectural language over the practical core of building by distinguishing the architectural manifestation of a sacred community from the reality of the massive supports.

Commenting on the importance of the slender shafts within the vocabulary of Gothic language, Joan Evans proposed that "the Gothic style itself was passing out of its first stage of architectural grammar and logic into a further stage when its architects had mastered the art of

9.18 Medieval architects added aedicules to the tops of delicately clustered vertical shafts.

9.19 In England the linear elements of the shafts and ribs began to multiply. Ribs, Exeter Cathedral, 13th–14th century.

rhetoric as well."[58] Individual shafts surrounding piers and other linear elements were multiplied and set into more elaborate rhythmic patterns of articulation. The ribs of vaulting were repeated many times, and archivolts were multiplied around openings as they interwove into the space of arches. "The tendency in England was to multiply colonnettes, ribs, and mouldings like the monorhymed tirades of Anglo-Norman verse"[59] (figure 9.19). Evans's reference to poetry is significant; we might consider the sanctuary of a Gothic cathedral as an

9.20 The sanctuary of a Gothic cathedral can be seen as an immensely orchestrated tirade. Angel choir, Lincoln Cathedral, mid-13th century.

immensely orchestrated tirade accomplished by chorus lines of gesturing bodies (figure 9.20). The massive piers at the base evoke a stiff regiment of upright bodies supporting the greater frequency of aedicular openings running along the second-story level of the nave. Perhaps the most populated and syncopated chorus of upright bodies occurs along those openings of the triforium arcades (figure 9.21) as they support the row of clerestory windows immediately above. Those ethereal windows distend upward through light to finally transform into the intricate traceried ornament at the culmination.

Both the classical and the Gothic feats of Western architecture evolved into rich and intelligible languages when their elements became conventionalized. As the Doric, Ionic, Corinthian, and composite orders were repeated, refined, diminished, magnified, and rhythmized, they became visual words and metaphors capable of incorporating ideas, allegories, and social rhetoric into many types and programs of building. Indeed, the classical language was so naturally understandable that it has perdured for over two thousand years as the embodied columns and their ornament maintained their empathetic authority in modern statehouses, museums, and libraries.

The Gothic language similarly endured. Although partly descended from the Roman tradition, it developed a northern European character and vocabulary. Its phrases—shafts, capitals, archivolts, pointed arches, and tracery—control architectural narratives ranging from the ecclesiological to the civic and collegiate. We can empathize with its aedicules, which are as basically human as the ancient column and capital.

In both the classical and the Gothic, the shape of the edifice may be understood as an architectural diagram of a societal structure and its cosmos. In the cathedral, a hierarchy of patrons, saints, and deity is portrayed within openings that also function as architectural units of space. By each sensing a personal spatiality in the architectural elements, we readily move into and psychologically occupy the fabric of the architecture. We grasp and engage the material building with a rich sense of being there within all its levels of detail and transcendent expression. The columns and aedicules invite us to move out of our own bubbles of space into the orchestrated dance within the architecture. In the great classic works, the elemental synthesis of body and construction constitutes the most fundamental means of architectural narration, in which the incorporate body allows us to psychologically *be a building* and the articulation of the idea of construction allows us to *comprehend the act of building.* Those two "essences," of being and com-

9.21 The triforium arcade is the area of the Gothic cathedral's most populated chorus of rhythmized "bodies."

prehending buildings, are prerequisite to the emergence of architectural ornament.

Like the narrative of the Turtle Dance, architectural ornament tells stories and memorializes things originating both within and beyond the basic organization of buildings. As many art forms illustrate, the dynamic body with its repertoire of whole body, manual, and facial gestures can be the catalyst of an expansive visual vocabulary capable of evoking all manner of things existing in the world at large, such as plants, trees, animals, water, shells, and storms (figure 9.22). We readily acknowledge the elaboration of body gesture in the art of mime as well as in dance, sculpture, and the more abstract figuration of painting. We can also find in architectural ornament its most rhythmized presence.

9.22 Rococo ornament can evoke plants, water, shells, and storms. Die Wies Pilgrimage Church, Germany, 18th century.

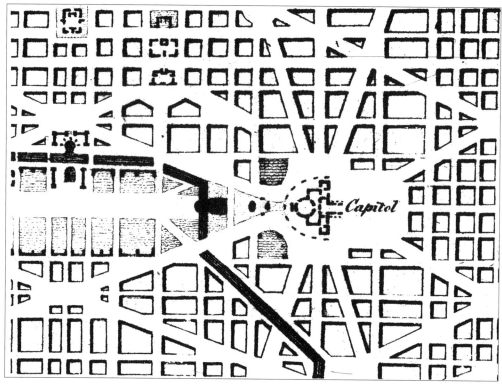

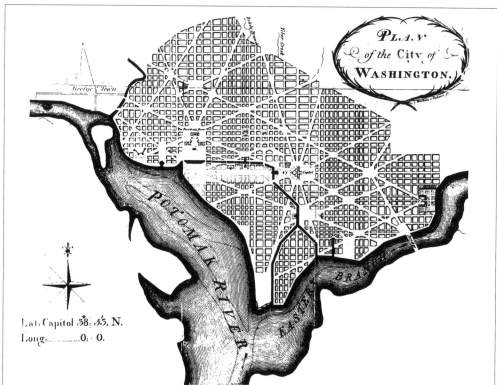

10.1, 10.2 L'Enfant's plan for the city of Washington recalled the architecture of imperial France and the plan at Versailles. U.S., 1792.

APPROPRIATION, REAPPROPRIATION, AND RELOCATION

It is as difficult to imagine how the basic grammar of ornament, particularly architectural ornament, could be reinvented at this moment in history as it would be to imagine reinventing the basic grammar of spoken language. Its vocabulary can still evolve and be augmented, resulting in all manner of new shapes and linkages with new materials and methods. But ornament's rhythmic structure, its mediating function, and its location within thresholds between elements of construction and space are essential to its identity as a distinct type of expression. Looking at the classical development and formation of ornament, we can discern at least its Western grammar in the making, with its ambivalent line work and its dependent nature. Although ornament's most ancient origins and its most profound psychological and social functions remain mysterious, its concretization into particular systems of figures from antiquity to the twentieth century provides us with an enormous and curiously consistent amount of typical material. In other words, ornament seems to have thrived upon a rather limited set of geometric, radiating, spiraling, and translating figures, which have managed to provide a large and nuanced family of visual ideas.

Great ornament reveals a disciplined and hardly spontaneous or ad hoc history. Indeed, Coleridge displayed uncanny insight (see chapter 3) when he located ornament as a stage of development between gesticulation and picture language. A review of the foliated scroll (see chapter 6) supports the notion that over time ornament thrives through a process of renewal, which includes borrowing as well as transforming from preceding schemes. It also reveals that different cultures tend to organize the most basic patterns of ornament in similar ways while simultaneously manifesting very distinct local characteristics.

Certain persistent figures within ornament, such as the lotus, the scroll, and the conventionalized wings of flight, have been appropriated and reappropriated by powerful institutions. By appearing to embody the power evoked by the figure and by impressing that figure into the ceremonial fabric of their buildings and public places, authorities have edified their dominions. But the appropriation of a typical ornament can rarely include a claim of origin by the appropriator. The form of the spiral, the acanthus, or the wing is not the innate property of any institution, although the association of an ornament with its previous claimant has always had a certain momentum over time.

Often after a conquest, a revolution, or the emergence of a new economy and means of production, the deposed emblems of power are discounted, vilified, and destroyed, or slightly modified and redistributed as symbols of power to manifest a new political order. For example, the political structure of modernity that commenced after the destruction of the French monarchy in 1789 raised questions about the importance and distribution of ornaments that were previously identified with the hierarchical order of the ancient regime. How could the new claimants of the public property conserve elements of ornament that were so closely associated with a defeated aristocracy in a society that no longer acknowledged their vertical structure of authority? Weren't the ornaments, their magnificence notwithstanding, still emblematic of an unacceptable tyranny? In the thick of those arguments, Quatremère de Quincy, writing in the French Academy of Letters in the decades immediately following the Revolution, perceived a threat to the entire legacy of art, and therefore ornament, were its fate to be placed in the hands of an elected administration dependent upon the support of multiple constituencies and competing interests. He argued that "the notion that the arts were a source of moral corruption because they served tyrants and despots and reinforced 'greed, vanity, debauchery, and the passions' neglected the true 'reciprocity of action between mores and the arts.' In a despotic social context the arts are as corrupted as they are corrupting and by implication in an ideal republic they are as virtuous as they are inspirers of virtue."[60] Quatremère saw in the captive ornament the potential of a basic language that, in its elegance, might serve the ideals appropriate to the architecture of an emerging republican form of government. He fur-

10.3 Stephen Hallet's precompetition design for the United States Capitol established the basic form of the building. 1791.

10.4 This design by William Thornton established the basic architectural grammar of the Capitol. 1793.

10.5 The two flanking houses of the national capitol were meant to articulate the American form of government. Thomas U. Walter, Capitol, wings and dome, Washington D.C., 1851–65.

ther argued that all the arts should be integrated and taught as a reflection of a "Republic of the Arts" in which architects, artists, and designers studied and worked together toward a basic right of free exhibition that he compared to freedom of the press. Quatremère had a bias for the language of classical architecture because of its sense of timelessness and its legacy of visual conventions in Western culture, although he allowed that other cultures with other beginnings might prefer their own original types. The modern Western task would be to identify or compose appropriate allegories for a republican society and to allow modern craftspeople and artists to express them in the language of a neoclassical architecture. As an expression of liberty, traditional ele-

10.6 The figure of American Liberty placed atop the Capitol's dome metaphorically replaces the statue of Apollo that was the supreme allegorical symbol of Louis XIV.

ments of ornament could act in the ancient manner to elevate rather than oppress the vitality of a modern society.

At about the same time, the American Revolution did not prevent that young republic from building a capital city and a capitol building that recalled Versailles and the courtly splendor of aristocratic French ornament. Thomas Jefferson had been minister to France, and some of the early planners and architects of the United States Capitol and its buildings were educated in French royal academies. Pierre-Charles L'Enfant's grandiose plan (figures 10.1 and 10.2) for the city of Washington prevailed, and French architect Stephen Hallet's design[61] for the United States Capitol (figure 10.3) established the basic form of the nineteenth-century designs by Thornton, Latrobe, and subsequent federal architects (figures 10.4 and 10.5). With its two houses flanking the central dome, the Capitol building royally articulates the new American form of federal organization. The disposition and assignment of principal spaces is designed in the manner of classical assembly halls. Upon the dome, the figure of Freedom (figure 10.6) stands in for the goddess of Liberty, which Quatremère had proposed as a replacement for the king's choice of Apollo as the supreme icon borrowed from ancient mythology. Moreover, the Capitol is ornamented with classical scrolls and festoons that harbor mythic icons in a manner that the seventeenth-century French court borrowed from the Italians. Whereas Louis XIV was symbolized in the iconography of Versailles with portraits of Apollo, "Benjamin Franklin had suggested the childhood strength and symbolic fearlessness of Hercules"[62] be represented in the Capitol building as appropriate to a young America. In homage to American agriculture, Latrobe replaced the antique acanthus leaves with spikes of wheat, corncobs (figure 10.7), and tobacco (figure 10.8) on the principal interior capitals. All of these new vocabulary pieces were distributed more or less in the royal manner, and the narrative power rooted in ancient Western mythology was still a vital source of inspiration for a country in the making.

This brief example illustrates the process of appropriation, in which key elements of the vocabulary are changed while the language and much of the grammatical structure of ornament are retained. To a large extent, the original and dynamic meanings innate to ancient ornament have been appropriated over and over. Political and spiritual contents presumably belonging to particular moments in the history of ornament have changed in ways parallel to the shifting themes incorporated in any form of communication, including musical and written messages, but the most basic figural repertoire of ornament (its

10.7 The architects of the Capitol building replaced the classical forms of acanthus leaves with wheat and corncobs.

10.8 Tobacco leaves appear upon some of the interior capitals.

rhythmized foliation, for example) seems to remain intact. Thus to avoid the practice of ornament merely on the grounds of its having been a property of earlier political orders or because it once contained alien "words" would, as Quatremère implied, only succeed in eliminating a basic and properly free level of human expression.

Unfortunately, ideals like Quatremère's Republic of the Arts were ultimately unable to check the questioning and politicizing of ornament that modernity has promoted. Two hundred years after Quatremère's warning, we still struggle with the problems of integrating art, history, and architecture and of developing an approach to ornament that may be supported by democratic assemblies. Those who promote ornament today are cautious about the legacy of its association with specific social hierarchies and the specter of material pretense. How can we declare a public landscape, a public building, or a public doorway worthy of special reverence in a country enjoying multiple political, religious, aesthetic, and ethnic values? Can the government of a multiethnic and officially egalitarian society point to moments, places, or even spots that are sufficiently "sacred" to warrant the extraordinary importance traditionally given to powerful ornament?

In looking back at the history of public space in America from the vantage point of the late twentieth century, J. B. Jackson observed some fundamental differences in the way that the New World, in contrast to Europe and antiquity, centered and "sanctified" places. "In Antiquity the holiness belonged to the place itself, and a sanctuary was erected there *because* the spot was holy. Zeus was surnamed *after* the mountains about whose summits he gathered his clouds. . . . *Place* in antiquity came first; the deity and his or her shrine came later."[63] In the Middle Ages, as Europe expanded to uncharted and unfamiliar territory, sacred spots had to be newly established in the light of the colonizing religions. "In Christendom it was the *action*, human or divine, that sanctified a place," and thus a miracle might precede the consecration of a newfound site. For Americans, occupying a new landscape lacking the original places innate to Western culture as well as the prescriptions provided by a traditional church and a monarchy, a place had to be sanctified by the placing of something there and *deeding it by word* to be of special importance. A visit to Mount Rushmore, for example, to gaze at Gutzon Borglum's giant portraits of five American presidents carved into the granite of the Black Hills of South Dakota effectively serves as a pilgrimage to a seemingly sacred site, though the "Shrine of Democracy" is less than a century old.

Americans have recently made similar dedications in homage to decaying monuments and main streets built and sometimes nearly forgotten by their pioneering ancestors. The practice of declaring historic works of architecture virtually sacred reached extraordinary heights after 1975 with the emergence of a publicly supported preservation movement. Key buildings, streets, landscapes, and cities have been awarded a status that echoes the reverence given to the sacred summits, waterfalls, and monuments of the European past. The demands for preservation after more than two hundred years of independence and unbridled "progress" have acted as the bellwethers of a public memory system. Fortunately, the respect for historic ornament attending the preservation movement has linked Americans with the architectural elements of their own past that they historically seemed anxious to outrun. As we associate the present with the venerable works from American history, ornaments may once again become active agents in our lives rather than being treated as relics belonging to a supposedly inaccessible past. Ornament, like spoken language, has always required the momentum of its own legacy in order to perdure, regenerate, reappropriate, and transform itself; and thus the late-twentieth-century failure to pay reverence to its legacy of ornament has until recently contributed to the weakening of the modern project of developing memorable places.

While the remembering of venerable ornament provides us with a measure of its original vitality, the imagining and positioning of new icons or "words" within ornament may provide us with a greater linkage to our future. Remembering and imagining have always been coincident properties of ornament. The metamorphoses and places of the imagination establish a realm of dreams that, by its aspiring nature, can become a form of communal property, or at least reveal the outlines of shared visions. However, the project of rendering dreamscapes in the tumultuous and as yet barely comprehensible space of modernity is particularly daunting as we move rapidly to construct altogether new settlements with little or no precedence of ornament in their immediate surrounds.

Yet new places for ornament seem to develop naturally along the thresholds connecting ordinary or "profane" districts to the spaces in life considered extraordinary. An approach to the modern sanctification of space in a developing and democratic social fabric is proposed by Michel Foucault in a 1967 article published in the French journal *Architecture—Mouvement—Continuité* in which Foucault considers the connections between places of reality and places of the imagination.

131

The article, "Of Other Spaces," focuses on the widespread existence of sacred spaces within the profane places that we continue to build. Foucault argues that modern space has not been fully desanctified, by citing the distinctions we make between family and social space; between cultural and useful space; and between leisure and work space. He proposes that these distinctions are still nurtured by distinctions between the sacred and the profane, distinctions connected by a kind of network that characterizes our epoch of "simultaneity, . . . of juxtaposition, the epoch of the near and far, of the side-by-side, of the dispersed."[64] Thus although "a certain theoretical desanctification of space has occurred, . . . we may still not have reached the point of a practical desanctification of space."[65] Because the relativistic space in which, theoretically, we live is heterogeneous and not firmly or traditionally centered, it provides us with a choice of *many sites* into which we may urgently move at different times and speeds. We may also oppose one site against another, or juxtapose one site with another.

Foucault proposes that today people seek to sanctify parcels of space in two fundamental ways. The first way is the attempt to create a utopia, which is a protected space destined to perish. That is, the utopian decision to sever a space from its physical and cultural context effectively rejects the instruments necessary to safeguard security, sovereignty, and practical knowledge. The second way is the creation of a heterotopia, which Foucault defines as being apart from but nevertheless connected to the ordinary spaces of the larger society. A heterotopia could have the features and the benefits of a utopia while remaining in vital contact with the utilitarian space of the unperfected society, "a sort of simultaneously mythic and real contestation of the space in which we live."[66] The tension of this contestation may be manifested in architecture by the architect's identifying and articulating the boundaries between the utopian dreams and the realms of necessity.

Foucault proceeds to identify principles with which we might identify heterotopian space. First, all cultures provide heterotopias in times of crisis, such as hospitals, prisons, and resorts. Second, over time the ideal location of a heterotopia may be moved in relation to the space of reality; for example, a cemetery once located in the center of a town may be moved to the edge as people's concept of the world of death changes. Third, a heterotopia can juxtapose several spaces that under normal circumstances are incompatible, as in the juxtapositions of time and position found upon the stage of a theater or the unnatural proximities of plants and animals found within botanical gardens and zoos. Fourth, heterotopias are most often linked to slices in time, such as those represented by the ever-accumulating collection of a library or the absolute temporality of the events staged within a fiesta. Fifth, heterotopias always presume a system of opening and closing (and here we might think of a ceremonial gateway) (figure 10.9) that both isolates them and makes them penetrable but not freely accessible.

The liminal space of the connection Foucault proposes between the heterotopia and the space of social reality corresponds to the typical place of ornament, which is between the extraordinary and the ordinary. Within its place, ornament mediates and articulates moments of transition between dreamscape and workscape.

While Quatremère de Quincy's Republic of the Arts envisions a coherent national place, heterotopias propose a collection of partially sequestered places interacting in "a sort of simultaneously mythic and real contestation" with the rest of the world. In this respect, Quatremère's skepticism about the possibility of instituting a *concerted* life of the arts in a democratic society was prophetic, especially if that life was expected to be visually or architecturally harmonious. Can we imagine a concerted art world in a society like that of the United States in which there is such a diversity of opinion?

Nevertheless, marvelous ornament has been distributed without interruption in many public or at least publicly visible and accessible

10.9 Heterotopias always presume rituals of entry and exit, as in this Soldiers' and Sailors' monument. Hartford, 19th century.

10.10 Ornament distributed on the exterior of Grand Central Station, New York.

projects conceived in the last 150 years. In nineteenth-century America, statehouses, courthouses, and town halls visually represented their democratic culture with its peculiarly eclectic character. The emergence of new institutions and building types that barely existed prior to the nineteenth century, such as public museums, monuments, zoos, and libraries, provided moments of exuberant and memorable architectural expression in urban and rural settings. Even in the private sector, ornaments distributed upon the facades and within the lobbies of railroad stations (figure 10.10), theaters, hotels, and office buildings (figure 10.11) built prior to World War II proceeded under the spirited direction of individual architects, owners, clients, and developers. More often than not, great projects of ornament in modern settings perpetuated the ancient function of centering and organizing the places in which they were located by infusing such places with the venerable voices and lively figuration originally conceived to do just that. Perhaps the reappropriated grammar and spirit of *ornament itself,* as much as the institutions, persons, or politics responsible for their distribution, have acted to sanctify moments in the architectural space of modernity by reappropriating figures of metamorphosis and the playfulness vital to the stuff of life.

But how has the intimate shaping of ornament managed to survive in the midst of modern industrialized construction, in which the details of building have become largely mechanized? Why haven't the engines of mass production completely overwhelmed the compositional intricacies, surprises, and asides to practicality that have always belonged to the life within ornament?

10.11 Ornament is evident within the lobbies and spires of office buildings. Hood and Howells, Tribune Tower, Chicago, 1925.

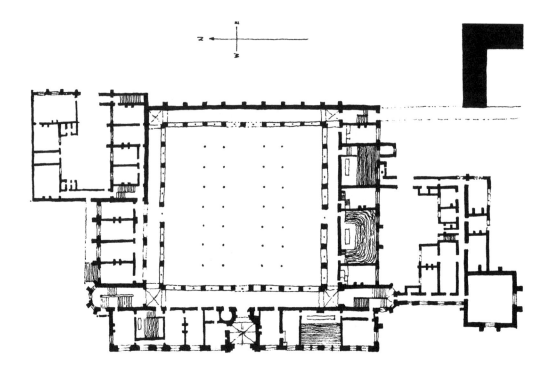

11.1, 11.2 Benjamin Woodward's design for Oxford University Museum was influenced by Ruskin's The Seven Lamps of Architecture. *The floor plan for the museum was simple and elegant.*

ORNAMENT AND MODERN TECHNOLOGY

For the last 175 years, elements of construction have been transformed by the power of engines and the increasing use of steel, concrete, and glass. The mechanized mass production of windows, doors,
wall panels, and moldings effectively reduced the importance and avail-
ability of traditional craftspeople, such as cabinetmakers, stonecarvers,
and metalsmiths, whose manual skills contributed so much to the historic shaping of ornament. Even the allure of timeless ornament
became diminished by a fascination with the polish of new technology.
By the twentieth century, bolts, I-beams, and trusswork had become
icons in the fabric of building. The champions of scientific and social
progress saw these mechanical elements as emblematizing the dream
of progress per se, serving as substitutes for the more typical and "premodern" vocabulary of ornament inherited from antiquity. A manifestation of that intoxication with modern engineering included the fore-
grounding of mechanical details which are seen by some as providing
a kit of parts sufficient to communicate the ideas central to modern
architecture. Others argued that restricting the expression of architectural elements to the technical facts of construction was somehow
morally correct, as bizarre as that notion must seem at the beginning
end of the twenty-first century.

A number of modern architects and clients employed the larger
legacy of architecture. They continued to explore the outer limits of
expression provided by ornament. Indeed, they combined a sense of
historic continuity with new industrialized means of construction without reducing the ability to express the basic facts of building or to exalt

the modern spatial forms of organization within the fabric of ornament. At the same time, they investigated, advanced, and deposited into modern design new technologies to fulfill all agendas of architecture. Thus in varying ways they kept in touch with precedent as they forged their way into the future, as evident in the following several projects.

OXFORD UNIVERSITY MUSEUM

The University Museum in Oxford (figure 11.1), constructed between 1855 and 1860, is a marvelous, perhaps somewhat eccentric example of the struggle to express new technologies of construction while holding on to the traditional scope and power of ornament. The design was influenced by John Ruskin's *The Seven Lamps of Architecture* (1849), in which medieval Gothic was cited as a supreme precedent. Ruskin objected to the geometric regularities he associated with classicism and the absence of artistry he perceived in the mass-produced object. He regarded Sir Joseph Paxton's enormous greenhouse, the Crystal Palace of 1851, as a monotonous work of nonarchitecture. At the same time, Ruskin argued against disguising the actual materials and systems of construction employed in a particular building. For Ruskin, a work of architecture above all had to express the sublime and beautiful works of nature, of which the building was but a moment.

The Dublin architect Benjamin Woodward had read *The Seven Lamps of Architecture* before he competed to design the world's first museum of natural history open to the academic public. Henry Acland, the principal client and a professor of medicine, consciously grappled with the problem of creating a historically new type of building to facilitate both the storage and exhibition of and the teaching and research about objects found in the history of the natural world. It was an occasion to explore the linguistic capacity of architecture in a manner that could present both the worlds from which the objects came and the urbane culture in which the objects were to be displayed.

Ruskin's theories about the beauty, power, and distribution of ornaments were particularly relevant because they were figuratively and intellectually rooted in his conviction that manifestations of nature revealed a sacred order capable of providing the most significant principles of architectural design. Moreover, a Ruskinian work of architecture would be a memorial to the idea that an orderly creation existed before the drastic human intervention of industrialization. This concern was poignant in the few years of the mid-nineteenth century during which the museum was constructed, as the debates flourished concerning a fixed creationist doctrine of natural history and Darwin's theory of competitive evolution. In *Seven Lamps*, Ruskin formulated principles of modern design that incorporated sculptural ornaments representing the local foliage and expressing the joy of the potentially liberated imagination of the modern worker. As a practitioner divorced from the more prescriptive authority of orthodox classicism, an architect pursuing these principles was expected to select elements from the Gothic language of architecture and to gather figures from the panorama of living nature.

Woodward developed a simple and elegant plan (figure 11.2), in which he posited an arrangement of piers and arches under a glazed canopy (figure 11.3) that recalls the sanctuary of a Gothic church protecting an arcaded courtyard. The two grand architectural ideas embodied in the Gothic sanctuary and the courtyard idealize the two worlds represented by the museum of natural history. The stone perimeter expresses the urbane place of public gathering, and the foliated glazed canopy of the sanctuary sanctifies the natural objects of exhibition. For Woodward, the pointed arches and their slender piers evoke the sublime forces of nature.

11.3 The piers and arches of Woodward's atrium recall the sanctuary of a Gothic church.

11.4 Branches and leaves spring from a glazed canopy suggesting a grove of trees.

Explicit expressions of stone, metal, and glass construction pervade the building. Arched exterior windows line the perimeter; polychrome arches and rows of metal columns and capitals occupy the interior gallery; and a glazed canopy covers the courtyard. Supporting the canopy, the slender shafts and metal arches of the interior "nave" structurally reiterate the ogival section of a medieval stone church, this time with the modern materials of cast iron and steel. To express the nature of iron and to conform with Ruskin's campaign against one material pretending to be another, Woodward dissolved the traditional monolithic form of a stone Gothic pier into bundles of independent cast-iron tubes.

11.5 In the iron arches of the museum, bold flanges and bolts perform as borders alongside delicate stencils.

About and fixed to the perimeter walls of the courtyard, standing at attention, a chorus of carved stone statues represents eminent philosophers and scientists, among them Aristotle, Galileo, and Newton, who seem to have succeeded the medieval saints. The statues appear to anticipate the visitor's inclination to gaze inward and upward to the crowning ornament, which is a distribution of branches and leaves (figure 11.4) springing from the metal structure within the luminous space of the webbing. In the ceiling vaults of the Middle Ages, webbing would have been filled with dark masonry surfaces; whereas in the Oxford Museum, figures of botanical nature suggest the living forest under a sky revealed by the modern technology of glass.

11.6 Each capital evokes a different plant in the museum's collection.

In each of the iron arches springing above the piers within the courtyard, bold monochrome flanges and bolts perform as borders alongside the more delicate polychrome flat-pattern stencils articulating the rhythms of stem, flower, and leaf (figure 11.5). This combination is in keeping with Ruskin's argument that sculptural forms are best rendered in monochrome and natural materials, which are sensitive to the movement of shadow, whereas sharply outlined and strong color patterns benefit from entirely flat surfaces.[67] At the same time, the crude three-dimensional elements of inherent construction along the flanges of the steel arches are exalted and slightly transformed by the adherent figures and colors of botanic nature upon their flat webs.

Beneath the arches are rows of capitals individually crafted to represent plants from the museum collection (figures 11.6 and 11.7). While conforming to the traditional classical and Gothic grammar, which placed foliated capitals upon shafts, the unique shapes and contents of the metal and stone capitals around the main court are the modern designs of James O'Shea and Company, in which the feelings and imagination of the worker contribute to the shaping of the ornament. Indeed, the O'Shea capitals simultaneously express a familiar article of history, a joint in the construction, a growing plant form, and the expressive personality of the worker. Their existence must have been a triumph for Ruskin, who, in *The Lamp of Life*, proposed that an amount of expressionism be added to the vocabulary of ornament as evidence of an individual's happiness inscribed by the quivering hand into a material object.

11.7 The plant capitals also incorporate the individual personality of the craftsman.

The Ruskinian grammar governing the museum is complex and rigorous. The result, in its totality, is eclectic and hybridistic because of the insertion of a modern glass-and-steel Gothic "forest" within the space of a traditional stone plaza; the building employs both traditional and contemporary expressions of construction. With a variegated tapestry of coincident details, the Ruskinian grammar challenged the more stridently geometric, unified, and homologous grammar of Greek classicism. In homage to a modern understanding of botany, the ornament incorporates images of local plants, in contrast to the highly conventionalized acanthus and lotus typical of ancient classical ornament.

A noteworthy American postscript to the use of literal meanings of the kind developed in the Oxford Museum may be found in a pair of "academic order columns" designed by Edward T. Potter at the entrance to Pecker Hall, 1866–69, at Lehigh University in Bethlehem, Pennsylvania. The academic building was to house a natural history museum along with chemistry laboratories, classrooms, philosophy offices, and a large chapel. While commenting on this building, historian Nicholas Adams points out that the

> historiated capital in the United States predates both Ruskin and Potter. . . . Benjamin Latrobe had created the corncob, tobacco, and cotton capitals in the United States Capitol building. . . . Latrobe's goal, however, was to duplicate the effect of ancient columns. . . . But for Potter, at Lehigh and elsewhere, the historiated capital and its decoration offered the opportunity to access to wider significance.[68]

11.8 Edward Potter's stack of books on Pecker Hall formed the academic order of column capitals. Lehigh University, Pennsylvania, 1866–69.

The capital of the academic order (figure 11.8) was articulated as a stack of books marked on their spines with the names of famous authors. Climbing from the neck and around the upper corners of the capital, laurel leaves clasp the books and burst outward.

FOUR "CURTAIN WALLS"

In Greco-Roman and Western medieval architecture, the erect column with its manifestation of vertical support and homage to gravity was an essential element of architectural composition that marshaled the rhythmic ordering of ornament. Columns and aedicules rhythmically connected to walls and canopies empathetically incorporated the occult human body both proportionately and imaginatively. The rows of humanized and visible building supports held aloft the animated ornaments of the mind, which almost always flourished in the upper reaches of the architecture. In other words, the fundamental expression of an architecture derived from posts and beams or arches was critical to the development of traditional Western ornament, as evident in the exuberance found so often in capitals and tracery.

With the advent of the regularized steel- and reinforced-concrete frame, especially with such a frame hidden behind the wall, the strong visual presence of the primary system of support as a muscular entity gave way to the more visible presence of an outer skin or membrane wrapping around a large volume. Such a movement from the spectacle of post and beam or arch to the flat, shroudlike appearance of a membrane dramatically changed the matrix in which the space of ornament could be created and into which the figures of ornament could be distributed. We might say that when we look at the mass of modern building, especially large buildings, we are looking at hidden piles of construction sealed off from sight within very delicate curtains.

The two distinct ways of ornamenting the mass of a building, one by the weight and muscularity of its frame and another upon the relative weightlessness and delicacy of its skin, invited a variety of responses.

Alexander Jackson Davis's study for the Astor Library, New York City, 1843, is as modern as it is classical. This simple structure was originally meant to be a library and a memorial able to stand firmly upon a raised solid platform, and thus Davis elected to design a coherent three-part arrangement of a pediment upon columns upon a plinth. The arrangement of structural forms into sets of three pervades this ideal composition within a taxonomy of descending scales from the overall composition of the library to the smallest and most subordinate architectural elements. For example, the supporting columns are further divided into base, shaft, and capital; the beam or entablature that they support is also subdivided into architrave, frieze, and cornice; and the architrave itself is further subdivided into three horizontal bands. In each of these triads, the bottom register is the most firm and the least elaborate, while the upper register is the most elaborate and protrusive. All the triads taken together belong to a system of homology in which a similar formation occurs at all scales. In the ancient classical manner, the basic triadic set functions as a governing code, a sort of genetic code, that almost always creates an upward transformation of shapes from the geometric to the organic. This arrangement produces multiple moments that manifest an allegory of transmutation from

11.9 In A. J. Davis's study for the Astor Library a triadic code governed the distribution of ornament.

an earthly to a more ethereal state along the upper margins of the major architectural elements.

The code also governs the designation of themes on the facade of Davis's study for the library (figure 11.9), the portico of which echoes the north porch of the Erechtheum in Athens (figure 11.10).

Three figures are portrayed on the facade: above the entrance door a bust, believed to be the donor; within the pediment another bust; and crowning the gable Phidias's Athena Promachus, representing wisdom and enlightenment.[69] The architect situated the donor in the lowest, most earthly position and placed Apollo in the lofty pediment, which, by its location in the apex of the temple, is conferred a mythic status amongst a haphazard arrangement of modern books.

145

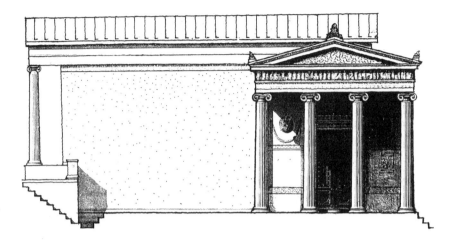

11.10 The facade of the Astor Library echoes the Erechtheum on the Athenian acropolis of the 5th century B.C.

Athena stands above them all, crowning the entire building as a transcendent presence that represents wisdom and the light of truth.

The foliated ornaments that embellish each of these portraits are descended from the scrolls of ancient Greece and serve to further exalt the donor, Apollo, and Athena within the triadic scheme of the building.

Starting below with the portrait of the donor, a transition among portrait, ornament, and utility occurs where the literal shoulders of the bust abruptly terminate and the foliated scrollwork begins to extend the outline of the shoulders to the extreme ends of the cornice canopy over the doorway. The canopy is structurally supported with the foliated brackets that effectively double as epaulets adorning the virtual body of the donor. The combinative figure of the door frame, canopy, scrollwork, and bust embeds the image of the donor into the facade and upon the ground, articulating the fact that the library was founded by the mortality of the Astors.

The portrait of Apollo is framed by a foliated cartouche in the form of a medallion that further encloses the god of the arts within the triangular frame of the lofty pediment. This respected realm of poetry and literature emblematizes the library's possessions.

Athena dwells above and beyond the building in a divine and supernatural realm. She shares the roof with acroteria that guard the corners and radiate the figure of the ancient palmette into the surround, as though mediating with another world above the horizon of the building. The goddess and the acroteria are connected the strident rhythms of a polychrome foliated scroll along the molding of the raking cornice.

146

In this scheme, the three portraits symbolize the three ascending worlds of the mortal, the ideal, and the divine, while the respective lotuses, scrolls, and palmettes signify the space and the sanctity of those worlds. Like the foliations upon the capitals that crown the columns, the scrolls on either side of the donor's bust, the medallion encircling Apollo, and the repeating ornament along the upper cornice and within the acroteria proclaim "places" that harbor the spirits of an allegory suitable to the idea of the library.

Some extraordinary features, not governed by the classical paradigm of the library's construction, are the virtual window walls that fill the intercolumnar space on the facade. This ingenious design of glass and metal mullions anticipates the technology of the twentieth-century curtain wall even as it reveals the spirit of an early nineteenth-century American inventor. It is safe to say that Davis's imitation of details from the ancient Erechtheum stemmed from no less a contemporary impulse than that which compelled him to preinvent the glass curtain wall. A curtain wall, unlike the upright physical structure of post and beam standing in the foreground of the Astor Library, is a membrane and does not present the upright hierarchies inherent to a post-and-beam structure. In keeping with the regular grid of the wall, Davis decorated the principal mullions with an identical repeating pattern along both the vertical and horizontal members. Subordinate to the mullions, he designed two additional and smaller sets of window frames, the smaller set being oriented along the diagonal axis with markings at each crossing. The geometry within the window-wall composition belongs more to an industrialized architectural geometry than to the triadic ordering descended from the wooden hut. In this respect, the primary language of the Astor Library is actually eclectic, or plurally "coded," as it unites elements from the refined vocabulary of antiquity with the less familiar and emerging expressions of modern technology.

In the Karlsplatz Station, Vienna, 1898–99, Otto Wagner also combined expressions of post, beam, and arch within a technology of steel and panel construction performing as a curtain wall. Wagner was an accomplished Beaux-Arts classicist who produced portfolios of elaborate drawings depicting designs at all scales from light fixtures to large urban settings. He was driven by a commanding knowledge of historical architectural vocabularies and a respect for new industrial means of construction. Together, these impulses led him to develop forms that were simultaneously traditional and modern.

The basic architectural element that governs the design of the

11.11 The basic element of the Karlsplatz Station is a palatial front entrance to the trains underneath. Vienna, 1898–99.

Karlsplatz Station is an elegant—indeed, a palatial—front entrance piece (figure 11.11) that clearly signifies a public doorway to the city-wide railroad situated beneath the street level. The imposing arched entrance is illuminated by two great hanging light fixtures and buttressed on both sides by small, somewhat cubical housings, or wings. The doorway and small wings form a pavilion manifesting an intriguing tension between the grandeur of the doorway and the smallness of the entire building in the context of downtown Vienna.

The slender lineaments of a prefabricated iron frame, the cantilevered slabs of flat and barrel-vaulted roofs, and the flat infilling panels of marble, stucco, and glass succinctly forecast the nature of panelized construction that was to become emblematic of the International Style of the twentieth century. The articulated lightness of the metal construction and the expansive panes of glass contrasted boldly with the weighty language of stone that dominated Vienna at the time.

Along with the new lightweight technology, Wagner appropriated and redistributed ornaments that flourished in the structures of antiquity. This he accomplished by ordering the building within the basic triadic system, in which the lower tier of panels is prosaic and plain while the upper transom levels are exuberant, foliated, and protrusive.

The most widely distributed figures are flowers, leaves, festoons, and scrolls. The achievement of the ornament in this project may be found in Otto Wagner's capacity to order a generous set of predomi-

11.12 Otto Wagner's foliated scroll along the eaves of the Karlsplatz Station is the most sculptural of the ornamentation.

nantly flat-pattern ornaments coincident with the new technology of steel and membrane construction.

The ornament within the uppermost register running along the parapet over the wings and along the fascia of the great arched canopy contains repeating patterns that recall the rhythmic properties of the foliation occupying the cornices of antiquity. The scrollwork along the eave of the arched canopy (figure 11.12) is the most florid sculpturally. Smaller scrolls cling to the upper corners of windows (figure 11.13), and along the glass windows and white wall panels there is a flat-pattern frieze that consists of sunflowers growing upward from a bed of vinage.

The sunflower is the principal icon that signifies the moments of efflorescence and acts as the climax of each panel. The row of circles along the frieze is reminiscent of Sullivan's ornament upon the friezes of the Wainwright Building of 1890–91 (figure 11.14) and the Guaranty Building of 1894–96 (figure 11.15). The inspiration of nature that infected Sullivan and the European masters of the Art Nouveau clearly was at work in the nearly contemporaneous design of the Karlsplatz Station.

Wagner also exploited the vertical expression of his principal supports. At the outer corners of the building as well as at the projecting corners of the main vestibule, the iron posts performing as mullions produce a forty-five-degree facet. Above the corners, the two slender posts extend upward into curiously erect semblances of an acroterion, while at the corners of the vestibule the mullions congeal into a thick column holding up the vaulted roof. On each facade of the wings,

11.13 A scroll proclaims a corner on a window, Karlsplatz Station.

11.14 Nature inspired Louis Sullivan's Wainwright Building, St. Louis, 1890–92.

three posts project upward through the overhanging roof to become finials doubling as fence posts for the parapet.

The vertical mullions appearing as colonnettes within the large glass transom cannot so readily imitate or transform the classical elements descended from the forms of traditional stone architecture. As they make contact with the great curved metal frame, there is no explicit transmission of support into the apparently self-sufficient and visually stable arch, and consequently Wagner terminates them with blossoms asymmetrically moving outward in a flourish of leafage that is echoed at their bases with an inward trace. In these colonnettes, the pervasive theme of organic nature is conserved. Indeed, Wagner demonstrates the ad hoc capacity of botanic form to signify transitional moments in the tapestry of a fundamentally modern architectural technology.

11.15 The Guaranty Building was also inspired by nature. Buffalo, NY, 1894–95.

Between 1950 and 1965, the ongoing development and production of major architectural ornament virtually ceased in Europe and the United States while the geometry of the International Style flourished and dominated the imaginations of architects in the advanced industrial world. These architects held that the traditionally rich vocabulary of ornament could be replaced by technological details and the regular repeating patterns emblematic of mass-produced systems of construction. Europe was still recovering from the devastation of World War II, and a booming America was anxious to tear down and make way for new building. Mexico at that time had not established an industrial momentum commensurate with that of the United States, Canada, and northern Europe, although many of its architects were captivated by the promise of a modern movement claiming to present progress. The basic design of the new library of University City, Mexico, 1950–52,

11.16 The library stack at Juan O'Gorman's Ciudad Universitaria, Mexico, is levitated mass upon minimal columns. Northern facade.

was international in style; its bookstack, a levitated mass upon minimal columns (figure 11.16) was cousin to the Lever House (figure 11.17), in New York City. However, architect Juan O'Gorman distributed an immense flat-pattern mosaic upon the elevated block containing the bookstacks that was a spectacular rejection of the gridded glass curtain that prevailed north of the border.

Mexico has a rich legacy of figural ornament and polychrome tilework, an amount of which can be traced to Islamic patterns imported by the Spanish. But it also bears the complexity of a truncated history in which a pre-Columbian splendor was replaced by a viceregal splendor, which was in turn overwhelmed by the industrial forms of modernity. In Mexico, distinct expressions of past and present cultures seem to collide both in fact and in the imagination.

As an architect, painter, and mosaicist, Juan O'Gorman was alarmed by the growing separations between architecture, painting, sculpture, and the crafts. It is puzzling, therefore, that a few years after he completed his extraordinary project of ornamenting the library of University City he declared,

> I think that the whole question of mosaics should be treated as an architectural theme. I find it is unfortunate that the interest in mosaics has been taken up as a billboard decoration for the blank walls of the architecture of the International Style, which is contrary to the baroque char-

acter of the mosaics. Let us hope that architecture will some day combine with the fantasy of the baroque spirit and that the influence of one on the other will produce a really great popular style.[70]

However, O'Gorman reconsidered his unhappiness with and criticism of his own project thirteen years later when he wrote that "there is no question that the University City gained, in interest for the public in general, with the work realized by the Mexican painters upon the walls of its buildings. This first step of mural decoration on the exterior of buildings has been given the name of plastic integration."[71]

In "Towards a Realistic Integration of the Plastic Arts in Mexico," a short paper written in 1982, he defined plastic integration as a condition in which "architecture, painting, and sculpture are realized in harmonious conjunction, as well as its character as a style."[72] Yet in the intervening years he witnessed a collapse of the initiative to integrate the arts realized at University City. He attributed that collapse to an inevitable conflict between the forms of the "abstract and non-objective class [of] modern architecture" and the images found in popular art forms that seek to express the aspirations and the life of the Mexican community. He objected to trends in art schools of the seventies to promote forms of abstract and autonomous art suited to the blank spaces of art galleries. He insisted that the rich figurative and symbolic "objective realism" found in works like the mosaics upon the library would lose their vitality if their style was altered and simplified and commodified. Almost as if repeating Quatremère de Quincy's early nineteenth-century concerns, O'Gorman observed that "within the capitalist regime, the arts are independent and each artist works separately on his work which he sells in the marketplace as an individual product. This allows a painting and sculpture to flourish that is made, not for a given architectural site, but to be attached to any place."[73] Architects, builders, painters, and sculptors were thus divided and their works subordinated to the specialized procedures of mass production. More than a century earlier, Ruskin had voiced similar complaints about the enslavement of the worker, in the "Lamp of Life" section of *The Seven Lamps of Architecture.*

In 1959, O'Gorman thought it was unfortunate that the "plasticity" of the mosaics had to submit to flat blank walls rather than more baroque and fantastical curvilinear structures, perhaps like the ones he designed for domestic patios reminiscent of the walls Antonio Gaudí designed for the Parque Guell in Barcelona. He also criticized developments in which some modern artists radically abstracted their work and limited their powers of representation to conform to the simple geometries of modern architecture, although it was obvious that proponents of incorporating "abstract" artworks into geometrically regularized buildings would claim that such a conformity was in fact a means of plastic integration. Yet, by accepting the flat walls of the book tower and by at least organizing the basic composition of his mosaics around the severely rational geometry and symmetry of the building, O'Gorman actually succeeded in producing one of the most powerful and memorable works of flat-pattern ornament in the fabric of modernity. Within the tilework, he made few concessions to the regular geometric character of the International Style, at least in regard to the graphic character of the myriad figures he distributed relentlessly over the entire planar surfaces of the book tower. However, the dynamic compositions of his flat-pattern figures upon the absolutely static geometry and symmetry of the stelalike slab seated ceremoniously within the campus seem extraordinarily suited to one another despite their "plastic" differences. The means of conventionalizing the two levels of expression in which figures and actions originating in the world at large are superadded to ideal figures originating in the construction and space of industrial building may be found in the agency of the flatness to which both levels of articulation make concessions. Here we have an instance of Ruskin's blending of essences as well as his approval of polychrome design on completely flat surfaces.

The primary architectural language of the library does not focus on the supports and material gravity of a large building. To the contrary, in keeping with other International Style works of that period, the greater mass of the building aspires to float free from the plinth upon which it is situated as though in defiance of gravity. That transcendent and ethereal quality extends to the sizing and visible location of structural members as well as to the use of glass at the base of the principal slab.

The robust distribution of tiles are reminiscent of the Islamic tradition, a tradition that influenced the architects of the first century of Spanish Mexico; although unlike figures in the Islamic tradition, and perhaps more reminiscent of the picture language belonging to the pre-Columbian Mexican tradition, the figures upon the library are glyphic, pictographic, and irregularly distributed. Flat-pattern ornament, particularly the Islamic, is descended in part from a nomadic architecture of tents and fabrics, which may be well suited for the distribution of patterns upon the taut surfaces of curtain-wall construction. O'Gorman "developed a technique of making

11.17 Like the Mexican library, Lever House was also levitated. Skidmore Owings & Merrill, New York.

mosaics in meter-square panels to be hooked to the walls of the building."[74] This outer skin performed as a wrapper rigged outward from the principal column-grid. Thus, O'Gorman's overall distribution of figures embellishes a modern fabric that wraps and encloses space. Even the vertical rows of openings illuminating the stairwells and corridors located behind the centerline of each exterior wall are "convened" into the figural composition of the mosaic rather than being separately expressed as windows or as a stack of corridors extending outward from the interior to interrupt the continuous surface of the exterior.

11.18 O'Gorman inscribed basic geometric circles of immense size on the southern facade of the library at Ciudad Universitaria.

Although the individual figures and the groups of figures in the mosaic taken one at a time belong to the rich and varied mythology of the Mexican community, O'Gorman sometimes inscribed elements of basic geometry at immense scales that are consonant with the shape and size of the book tower. On the principal southern facade, the two giant circles (figure 11.18), nearly four stories in diameter, belong to the scale and geometry of the building and appear to be the eyes of a rectangular robotic skull. The vertical row of horizontal openings between the solar eyes functions as the base and entablature of a church at the bottom and a temple between the fifth and sixth levels, allowing pieces of real and imaginary architecture to intermingle. A story-high image of a book acts as the crowning figure upon the elevator housing seated atop the giant bookstack. An immense shield and banner and an enormous figure of atomic energy center the western and eastern elevations. Other figures, including saints, stars, smokestacks, bombs, ballplayers, and burros, as well as trees and words, all seem to operate in their own graphic space while at the same time belonging to rhythmic patterns that reflect the larger symmetries of the building.

Octavio Paz speaks of the syncretism in Mexican art and architecture resulting from a necessity to unite apparently conflicting philosophies and grammars in order to fulfill all the agendas of a project.[75] The all-encompassing spread of ornaments encrusting the interior of the eighteenth-century church of Tonantzintla (figures 11.19 and 11.20) competes with the classical hierarchy of the basic architecture in a manner similar to the way that the engulfing mosaics of the library

11.19 Syncretism unites the traditionally conflicted elements within the iconography of Tonantzintla. 18th century.

11.20 The all-encompassing ornament of the church competes with a basic classical order.

compete with the customary austerity of the International Style. Both works of architecture were applauded in the twentieth century as being powerful, lucid, and eloquently narrative. Both are marvelously executed, the former by unknown native artisans and the latter by a sophisticated modern architect, ceramicist, and painter. If the authors of either project had failed to proceed on the grounds that no elegant unifying theory of design or grammar united the primary and secondary levels of architectural language—and O'Gorman suggested that in his case none did—we would be deprived of these extraordinary works of ornament. Yet the theoretical absence of a unifying system of design raises questions about the nature of ornament. Syncretism appears to work quite well when there are no clear alternatives and when the conflicting agendas are brought together passionately in the hands of outstanding artisans and architects. In both Tonantzintla and the library, coherent spatial allegories were achieved. Tonantzintla became a memory-cave, and the exterior walls of the library became a tapestry or stela capable of registering at once the cultural complexity of Mexico. In both examples, though, there was an established primary language of architecture. In Tonantzintla, a somewhat classical colonial grammar of church architecture was involuted with a continuum of intricate and thoughtful native relief sculpture; while in the library, a skilled painter-architect was set in positive opposition to the International Style, an architecture in which the decorative functions were limited to the rational details of construction. If syncretism as a systematic approach to distributing ornament in the space of modernity can be faulted, it may be in the observation that neither Tonantzintla nor the University City library gave birth to a movement or a series of ongoing projects in which their peculiar insights could be appropriated and further tested over time and in a variety of settings. O'Gorman lamented that fact before his death.

A great municipal library is a depository of manuscripts and themes that span the entirety of Western civilization and as such represents a large slice of time. The Library Center in Chicago, 1993, is also a memorial to the life and civic leadership of one of the city's mayors, Harold P. Washington. In homage to both of these subjects, architect Thomas Beeby recommended a classical grammar as the ideal means of distributing modern ornament. Beeby also argued that an established and venerable architectural language is necessary to articulate ideas rooted in *both* the ancient and the modern worlds. He also understood that today the figures of ornament must be familiar and publicly recognizable. Perhaps the Gothic and its mutations could have been adopted for the Chicago library were it not for a likely overassociation with the residues of a living religion. The perpetuation of ancient Greek figures in architecture for thousands of years has effectively made Greco-Roman classicism into the secular public language generally regarded as "classical," and thus some semblance and geometric authority of the orders must be maintained if the work is to be declared classical.

The classical elements and grammar Beeby considered for the Chicago library had already been partially transformed and developed in the nineteenth century under the influence of the European academies by architects who had analyzed the Roman, the German, the Italian, and other responses in the light of the industrial age. Moreover, systems of ornament developed by the Beaux-Arts had already influenced the architecture of Chicago and are to be found everywhere in the fabric of large, steel-framed municipal and commercial structures throughout the city.

By granting that a library is *both* a utility and a monument to literature, Beeby combined weighty expressions of modern construction with ancient expressions of Western civilization. His solution was to design an immense triadic structure of base, arcade, and pediment

11.21 The Harold P. Washington Library is both utilitarian and a monument to literature. Front facade. Hammond Beeby and Babka, Chicago.

11.22 The modern ornament on the corner of the roof pediment is an evocation of ancient Greek ornament.

11.23 The palmette may descend from the Egyptian lotus motif.

seated upon a footprint measuring 207 feet by 361 feet and rising 182 feet above the streets of downtown Chicago (figure 11.21), combining vocabularies derived in part from Greco-Roman classicism, Louis Sullivan, and the International Style. Lobbies and public spaces such as the auditorium are located in the base; nine floors of bookstacks are located in the arcade; and the administrative offices surrounding a glazed-curtain-wall Wintergarden are situated in the "attic," or the pediment above.

As in Sullivan's Wainwright Building, in St. Louis, the material expressions of the elevations are most massive and firm at the granite base (figure 11.24) and lighten gradually as they move through immense brick arcades to the glazed pediment above. The entire building recalls the form of a Greek temple, its columns replaced with walls regularly penetrated by enormous arched windows and embellished with vertical pendants suspended from giant festoons located immediately below a bracketed ornamental railing. A cornice railing occupies the horizontal band of space once assigned to the entablature crowning a colonnade of ancient orders. Upon the centers and corners of the roof pediments, immense metal ornaments representing the ancient Greek antefix (figure 11.22) and acroterion (figure 11.23) are silhouetted by the tips of a palmette that may be partially descended from a flower form symbolizing the ancient Egyptian lotus. Signaling the entrance and guarding the four corners are the figures of five giant owls emblematic of wisdom. A continuous foliated eave surrounds three sides of the library, uniting the antefix and acroterion and rhythmically mediating between the building below and an ethereal world hovering

11.24 A modern eave descends from the ancient foliated scroll.

above the life of the metropolis. The foliations are pierced by the finials of the vertical mullions acting as spears, recalling a design by the nineteenth-century German architect Frederick Schinkel. The spears signify guardians standing at attention along the horizon of the library. In response, the foliage enfolds and pacifies the military gesture.

The lofty pediment fabricated from the glass and aluminum mullions rises above the balcony, combining the technology of late twentieth-century curtain-wall construction with the more traditional expressions of masonry construction below. It is precisely in the modern industrialized fabric of the pediment that the architect developed the most vivid ornaments descended from antiquity. Although glass curtain walls are the prevalent and often the most unadorned products of today's economy, they have the potential to be fantastical in their apparent weightlessness and reflectivity. The familiar glass and aluminum elements provide an ideal material setting for the incorporation of birds and ethereal foliation that are poetically associated with the sky. Reflective and evanescent, the glass can call attention to the sky and perform as the substance into and from which the botanical roof ornaments may convene. Thus the normal curtain walls of today may be fashioned to contribute to the allegorical life of ornament even within a classical language developed in masonry.

Thomas Beeby insisted that the botanical ornaments must not grow directly from any of the supports belonging to the basic construction, including the mullions of the curtain wall, but rather must belong to the more abstract family of geometry that controls the plan and section of the entire building. He required that the foliation appear to belong to a transcendental nature emanating from the heavens rather than from the materials of the Earth, unlike the articulation of the leaves in the atrium canopy of Woodward's University Museum, where they attach and sprout upward from the trunks and branches of metal shafts and ribs. The leaves and whorls of the library actually sprout in both directions from virtual stems that are more horizontal than vertical and originate in the liminal space of the horizon. Separating the motility of the roof ornaments from the solid upward supports of the building established a distinction between the firmament of the heavens and the physicality of the Earth. This distinction privileges the ornament by giving it a world dependent upon yet above the cacophony of the streets.

Beeby's design also descends from the architecture of the ancient temple, a structure traditionally employed as a sarcophagus in which venerable beings were entombed. In antiquity, the miniature stone monuments were half buried in the ground, sometimes embellished with acroteria sprouting flamelike from their roofs. Regarded as forces of renewal, the acroteria rose out of the substance of past lives. In this respect, the library may be the most sacred and popular burial place of modernity. Here the voices, mostly of the dead, are contained in books deposited in a building embellished by figures of ornament that have shared their voices over the centuries with the authors and scholars of Western civilization.

A TOWER

The Nebraska state capitol, designed by Bertram Grosvenor Goodhue in 1920 and completed in 1932, is a four-hundred-foot domed skyscraper ascending out of the center of a massive two-story square plinth measuring slightly more than four hundred by four hundred feet in

11.25 The dome of the Nebraska State Capitol tops a skyscraper in the prairie. Bertram Goodhue, Lincoln, Nebraska, 1916–28.

11.26 The heads of Wisdom and Justice observe the citizens from the facade of the building.

width (figure 11.25). The prominence of a skyscraper atop a broad base in downtown Lincoln, situated in the low rolling prairie of the Nebraska landscape, is a heroic modern achievement. The roadway leading to the main entrance was intended to provide a grandeur belonging as much to an ancient imperial culture as to the recently developed democratic capitol of modern American settlers.

Bertram Goodhue did not formally study architecture, and in 1884, at the age of fifteen, became an apprentice in the New York office of Renwick, Aspinwall, and Russell. Much of his career was focused on the design of churches, mostly in the medieval style. He was an extraordinarily talented draftsman who, in his early years, spent many hours in Europe and America drawing houses, churches, landscapes, and cityscapes in precise and picturesque details, which included careful rendering of ornament. Through the practice of looking, drawing, and recording, he impressed great works of historical architecture into his mind. Although a master of historical detail and grammar, Goodhue, toward the end of his life, when preparing the designs for the Nebraska state capitol, began to lose interest in the letters of European styles, especially classicism:

It has seemed to the authors [of the capitol] that the traditions of ancient Greece and Rome and eighteenth-century France are in no wise

11.27 The figures of Power and Mercy complete a metamorphosis from buttress to bust.

applicable in designing a building destined to be the seat of government of a great western commonwealth: So, while the architectural style may be called "Classic" it makes no pretense of belonging to a period of the past. Its authors have striven to present something worthy of the high uses to which the building is to be devoted, an index to that which is within, a State Capitol of the Here and Now, and naught else."[76]

Unlike his early works, with their more orthodox use of historical detail, Goodhue's later works gradually eliminated traditional moldings and shafts. Particularly on the exteriors, their walls were often bare, with sculpture emerging directly out of the primary architectural elements. In the words of Lee Lawrie, a principal sculptor of the Nebraska project, "sculpture here is not sculpture, but a branch grafted onto the architectural trunk. Forms that portray animate life emerge from blocks of stone with usually no line to indicate the beginning of the change and terminate in historical expression . . . akin to the method of the Egyptian carved story.[77]

The commissioners of the capitol building asked architect, sculptor, and painter to form a design team under the leadership of the architect. However, in addition to this team, the poet-philosopher-anthropologist Hartley Burr Alexander guided the creation of the ornament. Born the son of a pioneer in Lincoln nearly fifty years before the commission, Alexander was principally in charge of inscriptions and symbolism and composed a narrative for the architecture. He stated that

> the first story, earth-clinging, forms a dramatic platform upon which appears, like the circumvallation of an olden town, the low horizontal square of the outer edifice. Within this wall-like structure the transepts shape the four courts, while at the crux the central tower sweeps sheerly upward. It is geometrically simple.[78]

Atop the buttresses on either side of the entrance are busts of Wisdom, Justice, Power, and Mercy (figures 11.26 and 11.27), whose

11.28 The inscription above the door creates a moment of interaction between the spectator and the watchful figures.

166

11.29 The sculpture of the "Sower" atop the dome is lifted skyward and gestures in all directions.

heads face outward into the city as reflections of the proposal inscribed directly above the doorway, "the salvation of the state is watchfulness in the citizen" (figure 11.28). The shoulders of the four busts stiffen the buttresses at the base of the immense tower, while their faces, looking outward, illustrate the inscription by exemplifying watchfulness. It is an extraordinary moment of engagement between a spectator and a work of architecture when, while standing and reading that inscription, one sees the buttresses of the building transform into giant figures performing the expected task of watching the landscape.

Crowning the narratives of Western culture, American and regional history, the principal exterior element is a fifteen-foot statue of the "Sower" by Lee Lawrie standing upon and lifted skyward by the dome (figure 11.29). That figure, besides representing the farmer, represents

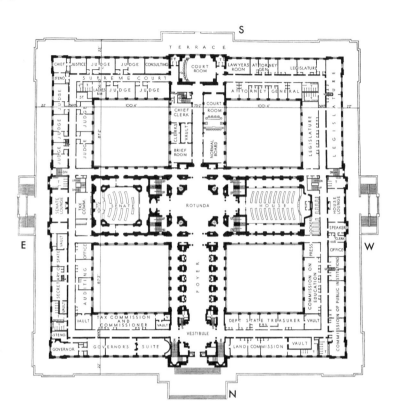

11.30 The plan of the second floor of the Nebraska Capitol is extremely ceremonial.

the government dispensing power. Wrapping like a necklace around the spring line of the dome at the top of the tower is a chevron fret and eight Indian thunderbirds assuring the fertile provisions of rain. At the ground level, flat-stone reliefs of buffalo flank the main-entrance steps, memorializing the principal occupants of the site prior to human beings' arrival.

The main floor of the capitol building is extremely ceremonial (figure 11.30), in that classical, medieval, Byzantine, and even Islamic vocabularies endow the principal passageways and rooms with familiar systems of ornament, perhaps more able to illustrate individual chapters of history and mythology. The mosaicist Hildreth Meiere and the mural painter Augustus Vincent Tack were given license to recount great memories and articles, from Indians hunting buffalo to Athenians discussing philosophy. The historiated limestone capitals supporting the colorful mosaic figures of Charity, Hope, Courage, Temperance, Wisdom, Faith, Justice, and Magnanimity are reflections of Greco-Roman capitals, their acanthuses transformed into corn, wheat, sunflower, and buffalo (figures 11.31, 11.32, and 11.33). The representation of local agriculture is probably more poignant for

11.31 Interior capitals celebrate buffalo and corn in the Greco-Roman tradition.

usurping the place of the ancient and conventionalized weed. The entire project is a cornucopia of nourishing and noble events from all of civilized time, honoring both Western history and the native people, flora, and fauna of Nebraska.

In 1924, four years after the Nebraska capitol was designed, the year of his death, Goodhue wrote to the English architect William Lethaby, "I have been working at architecture doing all sorts and kinds of things—classic, Gothic, and Goodness-Knows-What—and I still do. However my Gothic is no longer anything like historically correct, and my Classic (my formalistic friends deny me the use of this term) is anything but book classic."[79] He suggested he had achieved a "strange style, or a lack of style."

Goodhue was a great reader, admirer, and friend of Lethaby, who in 1891 wrote a seminal study of architectural origins entitled *Architecture, Mysticism, and Myth*, in which he suggested that forms and ornaments found in distinct architectural traditions were the emblems of ancient myths innate to particular cultures. For example, some of the flat geometric ornaments of Islam might recall the desert sky surrounding the decorated tents of an ancient nomadic people, whereas

11.32 This capital pays homage to native America.

11.33 Figures from the agriculture of Nebraska grow upon the capital alongside the ancient acanthus.

the leaves and branches of trees in the ornaments of a northern European society might represent the canopy above a people originally living in the forest. Goodhue, Alexander, and Lawrie were both adopting and creating myth for America in an allegorical language of architecture deposited in the wide open space of Lincoln, Nebraska.

Both Sullivan and Goodhue have been declared the inventors of the modern skyscraper—by American architectural historians Vincent Scully, who points to the Wainwright Building, and Richard Oliver, who points to the Nebraska capitol building. More significant, however, is that both architects developed powerful systems of ornament within new types of building with a clarity, grammatical rigor, and overall success that demonstrate that the language of ornament can be situated in modern building in such a way that the power of technology can be exalted rather than diminished.

I have chosen the six examples of architecture in this chapter to demonstrate that historical grammars and contemporary technologies can belong to singularly coherent and modern systems of design. In the dramatic combination of figures that originated in the minds and material cultures of our ancestors with the articulation of new techniques and patterns of construction, both the wisdom of the past and the wisdom of the present call attention to each other in a manner that reveals the dynamic phenomenon of change per se. Such an articulation of change may call attention to the shape of the future in ways that radically conserving the "past" or radically expressing the "present" by obfuscating the past could never achieve.

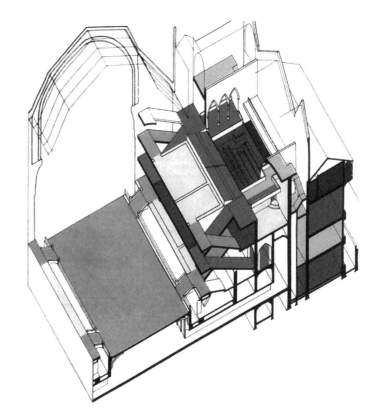

12.1 The plan of Alfred Waterhouse's Law Courts, London, reduced to an analytical diagram, drawn by the office of Sir Colin St. John Wilson.

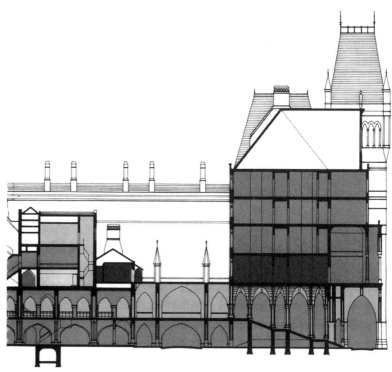

12.2 A diagram outlining the north-south public pedestrian way at the Law Courts.

ORNAMENT AND
THE MODERN PLAN

The focus on the importance of the plan and of efficient planning has become almost sacred in the practice of architecture during the last 150 years, as building has become more industrialized and society has become more complex and more mechanized. The human body has become less an icon to be celebrated by architecture and more an object or unit to be economically sheltered and efficiently moved through buildings. Indeed, by the mid-twentieth century the term *circulation* was commonly used in schools of design to describe patterns of human movement through buildings and streets. Meanwhile, the term was also used to describe the movement of automobiles, blood, and currency! Buildings were organized more and more as systems of conduits rather than as places of repose in which people could orient to the world at large and feel at home.

Some of the early masters of modern architecture even viewed the process of design as better associated with engineering than with "architecture" per se. Le Corbusier, in his seminal book *Towards a New Architecture*, first written in 1923, declared that "the Engineer, inspired by the law of Economy and governed by mathematical calculation, puts us in accord with universal law. . . . The plan is generator and holds in itself the essence of sensation. . . . The Plan proceeds from within to without; the exterior is the result of the interior."[80] In 1948, the influential historian of architecture Sigfried Giedion gave his famous treatise on modern architecture the ominous title *Mechanization Takes Command*.

To a large extent, mechanization had indeed taken command, by virtue of the mass production of construction from its components to its labor practices. Buildings with complex multiple functions necessarily required elaborate and rigorous planning. Moreover, the dramatic interweaving of "circulation" through modern buildings and motorized cities held a certain psychological appeal as it promised at first to provide more freedom, speed, and choice of destination and thus seemed appropriate, in a utopian sense, as the basis for an architecture standing for limitless, progressive, and democratic societies. Such economic realities and social promises, working side by side, managed to fuel a radical vision in which the manifestation of efficient "modern" plan forms would be exalted in a visually explicit manner to reveal, in Corbusier's words, "the essence of sensation." The expression of the plan as a machinelike element became iconic and acquired an enormous status in the determination of good design within the academies of modernist architecture, in which the first order of criticism frequently became "Show me the plan" or "Walk me through the plan." The radicalization of the plan-as-icon, however, has had a disastrous effect on the criticism about, certainly the call for, and largely the acknowledgment of ornament as a vital participant in the articulation of modern planning. Yet a walk through the history of buildings and building projects in the modern age reveals that ornament and plan form have often reinforced one another in projects of architecture resplendent with hallways, crossings, galleries, promenades, stairways, bridges, and tunnels.

THE LAW COURTS PROJECT, LONDON

The contemporary British architect and scholar Sir Colin St. John Wilson characterized the unbuilt Law Courts Project by Alfred Waterhouse, designed in 1866–67, as "an example of unsurpassed skill in the art of distributive organization."[81] Its footprint was to be greater than seven acres, located in the density of downtown Victorian London. The architecture was virtually a representation of a miniature city situated within an immense city. The constituencies of this "city" included, in the words of Waterhouse, the "general public," the "respectable public," and the "ladies gallery," as well as people involved in court, judges, lawyers, and a large staff including clerks and guards. In addition to twenty-four courtrooms, there were scores of offices, a major law library, and a Great Hall with a glazed roof, 478 feet long by

60 feet wide by 90 feet high, that could be used for general gathering and movement between court sessions.

The most dramatic moment in the planning of movement through the building was the intersection of two enormous passageways, one running north and south and the other east and west. They crossed at the geographic center of the building. At the moment of crossing, members of the general public moved fourteen feet beneath a bridge occupied by the public officially involved in court proceedings. Separated from those passages, as though belonging to another world, members of the legal profession moved through their own corridors running parallel to the public passages as well as about the perimeter of the building, where their offices were located.

With great ingenuity, Waterhouse accommodated the movement of all of these constituencies in a way that served each by providing the necessary amounts of privacy, semiprivacy, semipublicness, and publicness. The complex population of the Law Courts was intricately connected to the streets and buildings of greater London with bridges over the streets and entrances downward into three tube stations.

Had so brilliant and complex a work of planning been constructed in 1966, it probably would have appeared more like the analytical diagrams (figures 12.1 and 12.2) than the urbane renderings (figures 12.3, 12.4, and 12.5) drawn for the competition in 1866. The modernist version would likely have focused on the mechanistic expression of multiple pathways, while the Victorian version sought to glorify the civility and the splendor of moments along the pathways. The facts of "circulation" are the same for both approaches, the difference being in

12.3 The facade of the Law Courts from the Strand, rendered by Waterhouse for the 1866 competition.

12.4 Waterhouse's drawing of the interior of the Law Courts is a cosmic vision of practical space.

12.5 The interiors of the Law Courts are representations of the urbane world at large.

the mechanistic versus the humanist (or divine) visions of the world articulated by the architecture. In the design by Waterhouse, the facts of organized movement are infused with subordinate rhythms, visions of nature, echoes of style, and memories of human achievement. The adoption of a Gothic grammar reiterates the idea of the cosmic city in this modern setting; thus the project expresses the physicality of construction and merges that physicality with figures of ornament evoking the world at large.

STERLING MEMORIAL LIBRARY, YALE UNIVERSITY, NEW HAVEN, CONNECTICUT

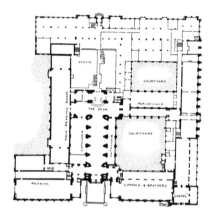

12.6 In J. G. Rogers' plan for the Sterling Memorial Library the major public rooms are all distributed on a single level. Yale University, New Haven.

The Sterling Memorial Library, designed by James Gamble Rogers and completed in 1930, remains a brilliant example of library planning and urban planning. Unlike its contemporary peers, such as the Library of Congress, Widener at Harvard, and the New York Public Library, it locates its major functions upon one integrated level (figure 12.6). The functional features include circulation and reference desks, reading and reserve-book rooms, periodical and rare-book rooms, public catalogs, lecture halls, exhibition spaces, and administrative offices. The fifteen levels of bookstacks are located in a tower reached by a centrally located elevator and stairs. This extraordinarily organic and efficient plan allows movement from one major room to another in short moments without the need for specialized corridors. Some of the regular patrons of Sterling wander over the course of a day in response to the trajectory of the sun as one might be tempted to do in a large private home.

The first plans for Sterling that Bertram Grosvenor Goodhue submitted coincided with the plan and massing of the Nebraska capitol building, although the dramatically lofty feats of construction are less pronounced in Sterling than in the capitol. As in the Nebraska capitol building (see figure 11.25), Goodhue situated a tower (figure 12.7) over a wide cluster of low-level buildings; because of comparatively lower height the tower looks somewhat like a truncated skyscraper.

The ornament of the library was conceived as a narrative about books, the contents of books, and the writers, collectors, and readers of books. In comments written shortly after the opening, Ellery S. Husted, class of 1924, declared that "the essence of a library is the bookstack, tier upon tier of self-supporting shelves with long slits of light lighting narrow aisles," and thus the great book tower "gives the library a structural dignity and direct symbolism."[82] From a great distance, the tower

12.7 Over the Sterling Memorial Library, Bertram Goodhue situated a tower that appears to be a truncated skyscraper.

broods over the entire campus, a monumental figure upon an urban village of collegiate buildings. The imagined rituals of monastic and manorial life are evoked through the planning of a modern library.

The main entrance portal appears to be ecclesiastical but actually alters the conventional form of entry into a medieval church by conjoining two entrances rather than presenting singular or triple doorways. However, by maintaining a sufficiently strong reference to the character of a medieval church, the entry facade invites the visitor to read a sacred narrative. Immediately surrounding the portals, the literacy of ancient civilizations is recounted with sculptures-in-relief depicting the history of writing. ("The sketch model was made by Mr. Lee Lawrie of New York City while Renè P. Chambellan followed this sketch in his own way in doing the full-sized sculpture."[83])

The entrance portal, the vestibule, and the main hall of the library appear to be in the form of a nave, with the circulation desk taking the central position of an altar. The procession of spaces provides a ritual of entrance into the chambers of the library. Located above the desk, in the most symbolic space of the nave, is a fresco enshrining the figure of Alma Mater standing in front of the tree of life and holding a darkened ball of light within a gilded aedicule. The ecclesiastical content of the fresco is subverted by the diminished luminescence from the figure of light and the rather earthly goddess's juxtaposition with a tree (figure 12.8).

Ten small carved reliefs depicting the founders of Yale carting books are distributed in positions similar to the traditional locations

12.8 Within the Alma Mater fresco, above the circulation desk, the traditional ecclesiastical content is subverted.

for the stations of the cross. Thus a traditional distribution of images descended from a religious liturgy is altered in content and appropriated for an academic narrative.

The form of the nave at the heart of the library has not only a religious legacy but also an older legacy descended from a "basilica," an architectural space used in ancient Rome for a court of justice or a place of public assembly. The medieval church itself appropriated the basilica form long before Gamble Rogers's appropriation for the central hall of a modern library. Thus the main hall of Sterling is most basically a typical element of architecture that has survived as a place of solemn assembly from antiquity to serve the gathering of academics. In just this way, the reappropriation of ancient and enduring types of architectural rooms is valuable to the production of modern ornament.

The plan of Sterling includes a virtual "tomb" and a virtual "chapel." The "tomb" is a reproduction of the Yale Library of 1742 and contains some of the original books owned by Yale as recorded in one of the university's first catalogs. The "chapel" is an octagonal and vaulted space of imposing height established at one corner of the library to enshrine the Gutenberg Bible, which has since been removed to the air-conditioned vaults of the Beinecke Library.

Flanking the main hall are great rooms, courtyards (figure 12.9), and passages, all of which are innate to traditional monastic architecture. Two of the principal reading rooms appear to be a grand living room and a dining hall. The "living room," called Linonia and

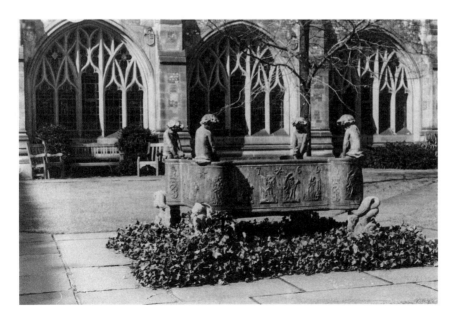

12.9 As in medieval monastic architecture, great halls and a cloister flank the main hall of Sterling Memorial Library.

12.10 The ceiling of the Linonia and Brothers "living room" feels like a turbulent skyscape.

Brothers, is manorial in character and is bounded by wood-paneled walls beneath a patterned plaster ceiling with a chain of geometric shapes and foliated drops animating a turbulent skyscape (figure 12.10). At the far end is a large noble fireplace carved from limestone, with two classically ordered columns holding a pediment festooned with animal skulls and harboring two large andirons with lion heads forged by Samuel Yellin. That great hearth signifies a private sitting place in which the reader withdraws from the noise and clutter of common life. Sleeping students appear to be retreating from the stress of academic life.

The main reading room, located diagonally across the nave from the "living room," is descended from the form of a monastic refectory. It is filled with the long narrow tables of a great dining hall, so that the act of reading becomes visually associated with a place of eating. The principal ornaments surrounding the reading room are seeds springing from the scrolls of a botanical frieze (figure 12.11) at the wainscot level above the bookshelves pressed against the wall. From the foliation of leaves mounted on a continuous wavy stem, grapes, acorns, seedpods, and pineapples emerge in a rhythmic chorus. Mounted on the cornice above a traceried clerestory, which is naturally lit from light wells and a courtyard, figures of medieval kings,

12.11 The botanical frieze, as well as the long narrow tables, gives the reading room the form of a refectory, allowing the act of reading to be associated with the act of eating.

scholars, and churchmen lean forward beneath a ceiling fabricated from 480 foiled panels clasped with gilded bosses and infilled with red and blue polychrome.

Although expressions of modern construction are not in the foreground of the narrative embodied by Sterling, twentieth-century technology is everywhere to be found (figure 12.12). The parquet floor to the main reading room, since replaced by a rug, was made from a synthetic rubber to silence footsteps. The subordinate mullions within the windows, which might have been fashioned from lead in medieval times, were industrially manufactured from steel in the form of operable casements. Within the bookstack above is an engine room of books, consisting of a steel subdivision of levels serviced by major and minor elevators and a warren of secondary stairways.

However, the brilliance of Sterling stems from the way that the architect appropriated rooms from a traditional vocabulary of architecture and *transformed their significance* to suit the spatial programs and narrative of an immense twentieth-century program of storage and research. Because the basic Gothic grammar and its monastic and manorial vision are poetically familiar to the educated mind, a visitor to the library can begin immediately to read the functions of the architectural plan. The traditional identities of the rooms can be readily per-

12.12 The interior construction of the stacks of the Sterling Memorial Library makes an engine room of books.

ceived, and the new narrative incorporated by the ornament can be enjoyed. The deity appears as Alma Mater, the disciples become pioneers and scholars, and some of the gargoyles become students. Ancient architectural rhetoric is thereby transformed into the rhetoric of a local mythology belonging to Yale and the life of scholarship.

In the realm of ornament, the architects of Nebraska's capitol and Sterling chose epic narratives embodying the history and ideals of their respective institutions. Yet differences governing their primary architectural organization had a profound influence on the kinds of stories each building is able to tell. As the sculptor Lee Lawrie, who worked on both projects, pointed out, the exterior of Nebraska's capitol wasarticulated with a minimal number of moldings, band courses,

184

friezes, niches, finials, and elaborations of ancient windows. Its plan is fiercely symmetrical. Sterling's plan is asymmetric and somewhat idiosyncratic. The foliated archivolts and tracery are more archeological and true to historic Gothic details than is the Nebraska capitol's more abstracted or streamlined joinery. The capitol's greater muscularity focuses on the enormous and dynamic feat of construction, like the great conquest of the western prairies. The colossal metamorphoses, such as the busts of Wisdom, Power, Justice, and Mercy upon the tower base at the north entrance, necessarily produce a heroic scale of expression, which from the standpoint of civic grandeur is a virtue. By contrast, Sterling's fussier, more domestic, more archeological, and more complex lineaments and breakdowns of scale and surface do not invite the heroic as much as encourage the distribution of all manner of strange characters, plots, and subplots that might be imagined in the sublime halls of a grand old house. The miniature carved arcades provide habitats for groups of legendary figures, as the roofscape above the giant bookstack provides a landscape for miniature temples and miniature stone towers. Bats, saints, reveling students, and mythic cities occupy the ledges and niches of a three-dimensional material work of literature, sometimes recording the solemn events of literacy and other times producing vignettes of the spoof and mischief allowed by storytelling. Thus the complexity and archeology of Sterling provide an extraordinarily rich and familiar setting for the kinds of multiple characters and scenes that, borrowed from Gothic ornament, serve well the anecdotes and myths of a modern university founded in the liberal arts.

The Carson Pirie Scott Department Store, Chicago

The gridded street plan of Chicago typifies the modern American city. In many respects, Chicago is the most modern of the great midwestern cities for having risen anew from the ashes of the great fire of 1871. The building boom that followed the fire developed so rapidly that the downtown at first became a mass of buildings without the traditional public spaces of squares, plazas, and parks suitable for public assembly and recreation. As a consequence, the ample streets, the deep sidewalks, and the street levels of buildings became the dominant places of public life. This crowded and thoroughly urbane setting was created coincidentally with the formulation of the modern steel-frame and high-rise building.

12.13 At the Carson Pirie Scott Department Store, Sullivan's ornaments are concentrated at the street level. Chicago, 1903–6.

Louis Sullivan won the commission to provide a uniform facade for an expanding department store at one of the busiest street corners in turn-of-the-century Chicago. With the collaboration of George Elmslie and the artist-craftsperson Kristian Schneider, he achieved the highest means of artistic production. The task was to design a nine- to twelve-story wall over and around several buildings of various heights to establish a single and coherent work of architecture.

In the Carson Pirie Scott Department Store project, executed in 1903–4, the ornaments were concentrated on the street level, in the mundane world of vehicles and pedestrians (figure 12.13), and reached a crescendo at the rounded-corner entrance facing an intersection of streets (figure 12.14). This design was the opposite of Sullivan's locating the principal ornaments on the attic of the Wainwright Building (see figure 11.14) ten years earlier or distributing them like a tapestry over the entire body of the Guaranty Building (figures 12.15 and 12.16). It seems that Sullivan was restoring to the groundscape of the city the primordial nature that had been devastated by the stupendous construction project that was the building of modern Chicago on the prairie. The architecture here manifests an allegory of a botanical nature positioned beneath a massive canopy of downtown buildings.

12.14 The ornament reaches a crescendo at the rounded corner facing a busy intersection.

12.15, 12.16 The ornament of Sullivan's Guaranty Building is distributed all over the body of the building like a tapestry. Buffalo, 1894–95.

However, in addition to providing a poetic vision of an earthly nature, there was the practical task of embellishing the ground-floor display windows of a department store. George Elmslie, a colleague of Sullivan's who contributed a great deal to the design of his ornaments, "has explained the conception of the ornament as a rich frame to a rich picture. The window displays were intended to attract the chief attention, but it was considered appropriate to frame those as beautifully as possible with a rich and delicate kind of ornament."[84] Thus Sullivan delivered to the commercial street level of a modern American urban plan the power of the foliated frame or cartouche previously assigned to the edge of heaven in the more prescriptive iconographies of premodern and baroque Europe.

The distribution of ornament in the Carson Pirie Scott Department Store reveals Sullivan's extraordinary virtuosity, his pragmatism, and the hand of an architect particularly sensitive to modern urban planning. By bringing the ornament into the base of the building, he ornamented the sidewalk as well as the building, a gesture confirmed by the frieze and protruding cornice atop the base between the second and third stories. In effect, Sullivan placed a high building atop a low building, with the low building belonging to the streets and the high building belonging to the skyscape of Chicago.

THE KINGSWOOD SCHOOL, CRANBROOK, BLOOMFIELD HILLS, MICHIGAN

Kingswood was founded as a residential girls' preparatory school in 1929 and planned as a gridwork of buildings sensitively responding to the landscape (figure 12.17). Although situated in a pastoral setting of gentle slopes, pond, and curving roadways, the modern organization of the buildings, designed by Eliel Saarinen, is disciplined by an orthogonal Cartesian system of coordinates upon which linear buildings are aligned (figure 12.18). Intersecting volumes form a variety of full courtyards, three-quarter courtyards, and individual wings housing major features such as the auditorium, the dining hall, the ballroom, and the library. The architecture delivers the low profile of a rural compound constructed from a variety of materials and structural methods, with some steel, some steel-reinforced concrete clad with brick or stone, and some masonry bearing walls. No singularly centered ordering of space dominates the campus. The profusion of pathways and sequestered courts and vistas defines

12.17 Eliel Saarinen based his design for the Kingswood School on a disciplined set of rectilinear coordinates.

12.18 In the plan of the Kingswood School linear elements are organized to form courtyards.

*12.19 In Saarinen's design of the
General Motors Technical Center
the diagrammatic character of
modernism is expressed. Detroit.*

an expansive twentieth-century scheme. Indeed, the gridded and
extendable nature of a plan marshaled by an orthogonal network
anticipates the abstract spirit belonging to the International Style of
modernism, a spirit more diagrammatically expressed in Saarinen's
GM Technical Center in Detroit, 1945 (figure 12.19). Yet out of the
many subordinate elements of architecture that altogether convey
an elegant, coherent, and homologous motif to the entire fabric of
Kingswood, a unique and powerful figure of ornament emerges that
punctuates, symbolically organizes, and thematically transcends the
rational plan.

That unique figure of ornament has the form of a ziggurat, with
successive stepped-back stages consisting of a sequence of similar bodies that are usually reduced several times in width as they ascend
upward, although occasionally those bodies expand as they ascend.
The figure appears to be an expression of growth echoing the bare
trunk of a tree as it narrows between major clusters of branches or
representing a sequence of calyxes along a stem.

The nearly occult presence of this botanic motif is immediately
established at the main-entrance gate (figures 12.20 and 12.21), where,
upon the piers on either side, finials that seem to be bundles of reeds
rise and curve outward in three stages, each terminating with a small

12.20 The dominant motif at
Kingswood begins at the main
entrance gate as an expression
of upward growth.

12.21 Upon the piers at the sides
of the Kingswood entrance gate
ziggurat-like figures present
a nearly occult botanic motif.

12.22 In the colonnade of the Kingswood School, flowers burst from slender shafts upon the primary supports.

12.23 The most extensive distribution of the stepped motif, introduced at the entrance gate, is found in the seven monumental chimneys.

face containing the figure of a leaf. The leaves spring from reveals in the masonry that appear to be stems emerging from the base.

Again, upon the shafts of the colonnade (figure 12.22) at the entrance to the residence, bundles of flower forms burst from the ends of slender vertical stems that embellish the three successive stepped-back stages of the column. Thus at the two principal places of entry the ziggurat form appears to originate in the natural dynamics of botanical growth.

With the plant form presented as a figure of ornament at the beginning of the journey into the campus, and through its constant while more abstract reiteration in the fabric of so many architectural elements from large to small, a motif is distributed into the rhythm of the rational plan that organizes the entire work of architecture. By becoming a repetitive voice that proclaims a dynamism and a respect

12.24 The stack of small half-circles culminating in a spiral at the end of a stone bench repeats the stepped motif.

for nature throughout the campus, the chanting ornament congeals the spirit and purpose of Kingswood's educational mission.

The most monumental and extensive distribution of the figure may be found in the profile of the seven chimneys (figure 12.23) marking the expanse of buildings. The rising and inward-stepping of a tall chimney is understandable from a purely utilitarian standpoint, but at Kingswood the form is clearly iconic and functions as an evocation of life-forms overtly impressed into a familiar architectural element that originally rose above the communal hearth.

The telescoping piers under the covered walkway and the supports of the light standards in the courtyards and terraces carry the stepped motif into outdoor spaces with more or less degrees of abstraction and conventionalization. Even the small stack of half-circles culminating in a spiral on the armrests in a stone bench (figure 12.24), designed by the sculptor Carl Milles, and patterns of brickwork (figure 12.25) incorporate the stepped motif.

In the leaded-glass window wall (figure 12.26) of an interior hallway, the basic geometric form is repeated twenty-five times. In the grillwork of the auditorium's ceiling heating register (figure 12.27), it appears rhythmically as a structural detail. The stacked metal cones of inverted lampshades (figure 12.28) and patterns running vertically up the folds of the stage curtain in the auditorium bring the changing motif into the furnishings of the school.

There are even stepped formations in the ribbing of the cast-concrete ceiling over the original weaving studio (figure 12.30); but on the

12.25 The patterns of the brickwork incorporate the stepped motif as well.

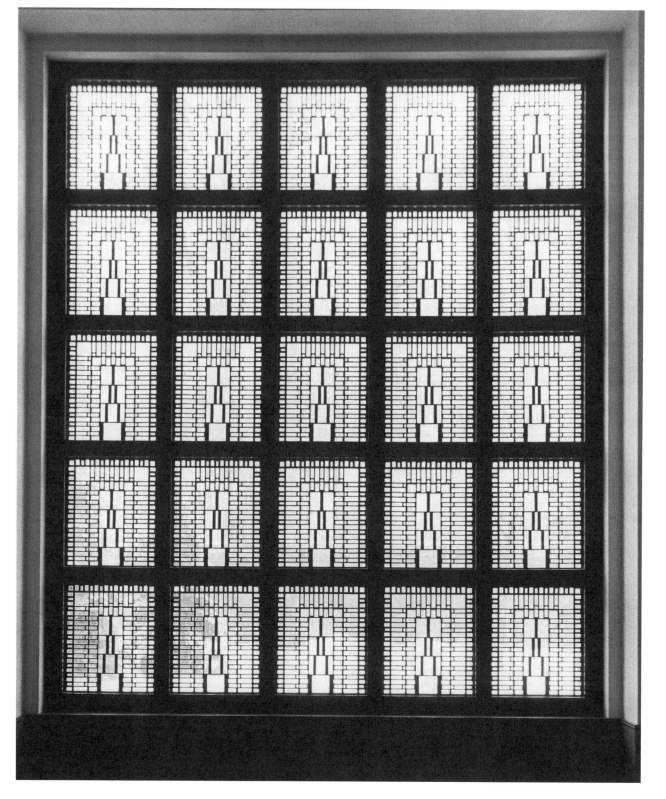

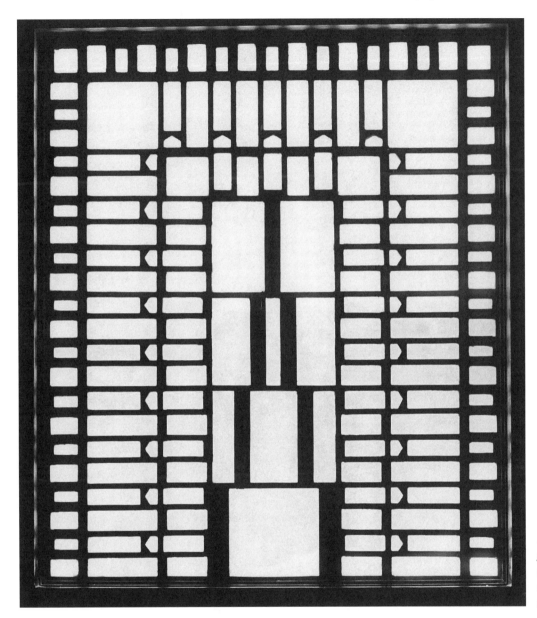

*12.27 The detailed
grillwork of the
auditorium's heating
register incorporates
the basic figure.*

*12.26 In the leaded-glass window of
an interior hallway, a basic geometric
form is repeated, also incorporating
the stepped motif.*

*12.28 Furnishings like
these floor lamps by the
young Eero Saarinen
echo the architecture.*

12.29 The overall motif is repeated in the individual window elements, here in the lobby entrance.

12.30 Even the concrete ceilings manage to incorporate the motif.

whole, the most dynamic figures of ornament are impressed into the more individuated elements and furnishings distributed throughout the entire plan of the building complex (figure 12.29). Indeed, the authority realized by the multiple incorporations of ornament in the minor elements is achieved by ingeniously springing the basic motif out of the everyday utilitarian objects. Certainly, the superb craft and material refinement lend substance to the architecture, but without the adherent form within the ornament the educational mission could not have been so fully and memorably expressed.

THE LEWIS THOMAS LABORATORY, PRINCETON UNIVERSITY, NEW JERSEY

The Lewis Thomas Laboratory, a molecular-biology research facility, was built at Princeton University in 1986. The interior of the building was planned by Payette Associates, a firm possessing years of experience with the pragmatics of laboratory design. As though recalling Sigfried Giedion's pronouncement nearly forty years earlier that mechanization takes command, Princeton almost allowed the building of an actual machine in the University garden. That is, the plan governing the form of the laboratory, necessarily rooted in a mechanistic efficiency, included an immense, windowless machinery loft in the attic above long regular rows of laboratories and offices.

12.31 In his design for the Lewis Thomas Laboratory, Robert Venturi exploited the immense size of the attic level as a place for a checkerboard motif.

12.32 The shallow arch above the entrance evokes the stonework of another time.

12.33 This entrance portico to several shops in 19th-century Stonington also celebrates the public domain by using ceremonial elements of architecture formulated in the past by another culture.

Robert Venturi accepted the severity and regularity of the plan as a condition of his design. He exploited the bigness of the attic as a place for a flat-pattern checkerboard motif (figure 12.31). The lofty grid pattern, which is antithetical to the human scale, comments on the absence of people up there and seems to throw the attic and its hidden machinery above the familiar realm of habitation. The big and abnormal checkerboard simultaneously calls attention to the presence of a rather normal building constituting the first three levels. Indeed, the representation of a normal building down there is articulated by the zigzag diaper patterns impressed upon the horizontal brick banding beneath and above the second level that is descended from a traditional pattern reminiscent of English manorial brickwork often employed in collegiate Gothic. By representing an element of the collegiate language prevalent on the Princeton campus, the bottom half of the laboratory joins the extended family of university buildings.

The shallow ogival arch (figure 12.32) suspended above the entrance is an evocative thing, a quotation from another time that serves to embellish the space of entry. It is also an ornament and a metamorphosis referring to forms of construction that originated in the statics of masonry construction, although Venturi's arch actually belongs more to curtain-wall construction than to upright stone construction, as it is severed from any visible supports below. In this respect, the expression of an opening descended from medieval construction in the Lewis Thomas Laboratory is a ceremonial idea about entry somewhat akin to the classical expressions of Doric columns at the entrance to a nineteenth-century shopping arcade in Stonington, Connecticut (figure 12.33). Although it could be argued that Venturi's arches are not really ornaments because they are descended from elements of architectural language that are innate to the inherent facts of construction, the degree to which they divorce themselves from the actual support system or framing within the laboratory building suggests otherwise. Unlike the Stonington columns, these arches are rhetorical for seeming to hang down from the attic rather than spring up from the ground. As with the traceries of the great medieval windows, in which the columns and arches disrupt terrestrial laws as they spin, cycle, and levitate in the liminal spaces of architecture, the physics of Venturi's arches are apprehended *into* rather than elaborated *out of* the basic facts of construction as they pay homage to the entryway rather than to the terrestrial laws of physics.

The arches behave as figures of ornament emerging upward from down low out of the rhythms that suffuse the building. In a curious way, they exalt the machinery in the attic as they tamper with the conventional expressions of earthly architectural structure. Admittedly, they are quite minimal, but they were designed in a period of architecture that had all but extinguished ornament as a living property of design. As such, the arches of the Lewis Thomas Laboratory perform like embers waiting to be fanned into flame. Indeed, I would have been delighted to see more evidence of inverted tracery issuing from their moldings. But certainly they work against that numbness so often felt from the tyranny of a building that merely expresses a reasonable plan made material and equipped with drab doors completely lacking ornament.

13.1 Buildings on the East Campus of the University of Texas at Austin built in the 1960s. The brick box is the Archer M. Huntington Art Gallery.

ON THE ABSENCE
OF ORNAMENT

[The] absence of ornament serves as much
as regular horizontality to differentiate
superficially the current style from the styles
of the past.

Henry-Russell Hitchcock and Philip Johnson[85]

The respect for history, mythology, and ornament that held the
center of nineteenth-century theory and much of early twentieth-century
practice in architecture was clouded by a malaise that began after
World War I and culminated after World War II. Much has been written
about the linkage between the social, political, and industrial crises
of those periods and the emergence of a revolutionary and antihistorical
"modernist" architectural movement that dominated the last half
of the twentieth century. Many have suggested that the history of architectural
ornament was ending by the time of the modernist project,
when a theoretically more "progressive," more mechanized, and
"purer" form of architecture seemed to take command (figure 13.1).

As the twenty-first century begins, it is evident that the knowledge
required to produce ornament belonging to our age cannot spontaneously
emerge. While the impulse to ornament may be intuitive, while
we can readily afford ornament, and while there are any number of
craftspeople, architects, painters, and sculptors willing to begin work
on it, the language of ornament, like the languages of speech and
music, must be nourished by active procedures of renewal and education.
There is simply not enough time within each successive generation
of designers and artisans to reinvent the complex grammar and
visual eloquence that are manifest in the most outstanding projects
from the past. The foliated scroll and great works of tracery were developed
over centuries, and the appearance of "new" forms of rhythmized
figurations always depended upon previous successes, formulas, and

failures over a long period of time. Indeed, the absence of ornament results from the absence of education about ornament, whether from the guild or from the academy.

Since this book is about the nature of ornament, I won't digress by analyzing the theoretical and political arguments that led to the avoidance and pejorative treatment of ornament within the modernist academies of design. However, as a teacher of ornament in a graduate school of architecture, I recognize the importance of identifying and criticizing the common reasons given for avoiding and even condemning ornament.

In the many years I have lectured on the subject, I have collected a list of canonlike prejudices that, often masquerading as truths, are constantly reiterated in the classroom as acceptable grounds for rejecting ornament. Such rejection is less evident in public or general nonacademic discourse. At the same time, there has been a dearth of rigorous argument in favor of the public value or function of these negations. Even when reasons are provided for opposing ornament, they usually are untested, quasi-moral, presumptive, and without regard for the fact that many people enjoy ornament. As a consequence, I regard the negativity toward the subject as more a fear, even a pathology, than a profound consideration. I often am intrigued by the psychological forces that motivate such opposition. Occasionally, I feel like an anthropologist investigating some odd and repressive culture.

No reason stands out above the others. Rather, the list in its canonized form is a compilation of questionable prejudices, all of which invite skepticism. At the same time, however, such a list of negations can indirectly shed light on the deepest nature of ornament, because by sensing what is opposed, we begin to see the outline and consequences of living in a world lacking ornament.

In this chapter, therefore, I present a summary of the most common articles of opposition, accompanied by my own responses based on the contents of the earlier chapters. I also ruminate about the consequences of building a world devoid of ornament. I ask the reader to understand that this list is didactic, developed from the forum of teaching in a modern professional school of architecture, and presented in no particular order.

1. Ornament is dishonest because it contains forms that are adherent to the basic facts of construction. Unlike sculpture and painting, architecture is the "art of building" and should confine its medium to those elements that denote the true physical structure. We should not be deceived.

This prejudice assumes that clients, occupants, and beholders are interested exclusively in the tectonics of architecture. On a larger scale, it implies that the principal icon in our cities, the building, ought to be rooted in a display of construction. Stated in somewhat nineteenth-century terms, this notion declares that the "subject" of the building should be expressed in the details that reveal a *material building* and that other, more narrative subjects of expression (figure 13.2, 13.3), rooted in memory, spirit, and history, are comparatively less important. Even to the extent that these other subjects are granted to be important, the "honest" approach would be to encode their immaterial character within a tectonic kit of parts that remain recognizable as structural elements. In the light of the figural complexity and history of ornament, this idea proposes a drastic limitation on the kind and scope of narrative figuration available to architectural language. Even our interior spaces would thus be designed only with economic elements and not with the uneconomic figures that evoke the nontectonic shapes of dreams so crucial to civilization. Ironically, it has been demonstrated for centuries that ornament, while reaching outward to the world beyond the building, has always simultaneously exalted basic construction by tapping its energy and exploring its edges.

Perhaps the very way that ornament goes about exalting the "honest" elements invites the charge of deception. When ornament appears within the liminal zones of construction, it produces an expression of metamorphosis. The "honest" element is momentarily disrupted and transformed into something else, such as the leafage upon a Corinthian capital, and thus the phenomenon of transformation displaces the pure expression of construction. This change threatens to become the principal essence in the perception of the entire composition. Never mind that the elements of basic construction are still visible, intact, and often made even more visible by virtue of the concentration of visual energy at one of their acute moments of joinery; the expression of metamorphosis itself remains an allusion rather than a true and factual explication of the material structure. James Trilling underscores this issue by saying that the artifice of "transformation . . . can tempt and deceive by offering an alternative to reality."[86] The figure of transformation, he explains, is perceived as a sort of monstrosity that defies the laws of nature.

But we must ask, as does Trilling, what reality and what laws are being defied? Such transformations have appeared in Western art for thousands of years and seem to have come under suspicion only through the search for purity of architectural expression based on a need for stating facts about materials and technology. If we point to an actual material or system of construction and say with assurance what the material is and how it is fabricated, then we know what is *going on* and thus are protected from whatever threat may be present in "a deformity and portent of chaos."[87] We are home safe in a well-ordered and predictable world.

But such a safe world, if taken too seriously, is a rather small one, dependent for its reality on a limited set of axioms. While the direct material truths are indeed truths of a kind, they are not the only truths by which we grow and establish our orientation to the world. Our memories and imaginations extend to realms, including material ones, beyond the building. As Donald Winnicott points out, we cannot even develop ourselves or our cultures without periodic movements into psychological spheres and moments of transition. These are the vital in-between spaces of nonnegation. Such in-between spaces are the limited domains of ornament, which if distributed carefully do not displace the domain of utilitarian reality but enhance it. The "honest" stuff is still there for anyone to look at and, ironically, if unrelieved might in its own limited way prove to be the more threatening.

2. Architecture today is primarily about space. It is by the expression of space that architecture can articulate worldly things. Ornament, on the other hand, has to do with nonspatial figuration and extraneous detail.

This proposition assumes that ornament does not directly address and condition the perception of space, an assumption perhaps reinforced by the absence of studies about the engagement between space and ornament. In theories of ornament that proliferated in the nineteenth century, it was generally assumed that ornament embellished construction; of course, the term *space* had not become as critical to theories of architecture as it did in the twentieth century. Yet ornament is fundamentally implicated with spatial form, particularly spatial boundaries (figure 13.4), as is evident by its traditional distribution into margins such as those between inside and outside (entries), along the upper edges of walls (Gothic tracery, classical friezes), and as the marking of center places (hearths, obelisks). Moreover, there is no such thing as "space" acting independently of physical form, unless we regard it as an independent gaseous substance flowing through the universe or as some kind of massive vacuum. Architectural space is not created by space. It is defined and qualified by the physical elements with which it is implicated, and that must include all aspects of those elements, from their base material to their ornament.

13.2, 13.3, 13.4 Details from Sutton Hall, designed in 1917 by Cass Gilbert as the education department, on the West Campus of the University of Texas at Austin.

Perhaps the most powerful contribution ornament makes to the articulation of architectural space is its capacity to transform the raw dimentions into a fantastic place. Ornament can evoke different magnitudes of scale, from the miniature to the magnificent. It can visually disrupt the static authority of a specific volume of space as it suggests rhythms and destinations inside and beyond its denotative boundaries.

3. The aesthetic functions of ornament can be "abstracted" and subsumed into the practical details of basic building.

Some of the aesthetic agendas belonging to systems of ornament can be distributed into the details of the basic building, but that does not mean that ornament per se can be subsumed. The phenomenon of ornament is not limited to its aesthetic function any more than the phenomenon of architecture is so limited, at least if we define the sensuous and pleasurable properties of design as the "aesthetic" ones. But such properties present only a part of ornament's agendas, the others being more precisely linguistic, with their allegiance to expressions of utility as well as, for example, meaningful evocations of society, myth, and nature. Thus while the linguistic agendas in ornament can be implicated with aesthetics, they cannot be reduced to a purely aesthetic function, because they have an additional narrative function. In this respect, the philosopher Karsten Harries makes a crucial distinction between ornament and decoration when he states that "from now on I shall call decoration that articulates a communal ethos *ornament* and decoration that we experience primarily as an aesthetic addition to building *decoration*. So understood decoration is the aesthetic analogue to ornament."[88] This proposition requires that expressions of communal ethos must be added to mere aesthetics (and hence superadded to utility) in order to produce ornament.

The aesthetic properties of ornament could be separated out, and these properties could be abstracted and subsumed into the practical details of basic building, but such an operation is not a substitute for ornament per se.

4. The entire building can be an ornament. There is no need to "superadd" ornament.

Thomas Beeby, in a paper begun in 1965 and subsequently entitled "The Grammar of Ornament, Ornament as Grammar," notes that Wright, Mies, and Le Corbusier, among others, attempted to construct "ornament" as the ordinate rather than the subordinate agenda of architecture. He cites a prophetic lecture delivered in 1869 by the English architect and critic Robert Kerr that distinguished between *structure ornamented*, that is, ornament superadded to the structural elements of architecture, and *ornament constructed*, in which the basic plans and structural elements are arranged to become the predominant figures of ornamental expression.

Beeby observes that after World War I modernist designers routinely moved away from the notion of "structure ornamented" to a pro-

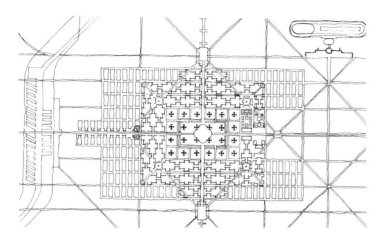

13.5 Le Corbusier's plan of 1922 incorporates into the plan of the city patterns that are visible from the sky.

cedure approaching that of "ornament constructed," in which the entire design process would begin within a geometry belonging to an ornamental pattern, such as a repetitive grid, rather than within a more historic or even more pragmatic means of organization. Large structural and spatial elements rather than subordinate ornaments were bent into systems of repeats, or symmetry patterns. Beeby illustrates Corbusier's plan of 1922 (figure 13.5) for a city of three million inhabitants, the center of which appears from the sky to be an emblem decoratively centered within the space of a diaper pattern. He also compares Wright's method of developing the entire plan of the Unity Temple to Sullivan's method of generating a particular ornament like the one illustrated in Sullivan's last book, *A System of Architectural Ornament,* called the "awakening of the pentagon" (figure 13.6),

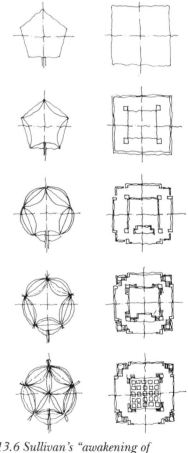

13.6 Sullivan's "awakening of the pentagon" illustrates a system of designing ornament.

13.7 Wright applied Sullivan's process in his design for the body of the Unity Temple.

13.8 The upper exterior piers of the Unity Temple provide an example of "structure ornamented," while the body of the Temple exemplifies "ornament constructed."

although in the process of designing Unity, Wright began with a cube rather than a pentagon and extended the figure much further into the three-dimensional shapes of a building (figure 13.7). It is important to note that the Unity Temple also provides "structure ornamented" on the upper pilasters of the exterior elevation (figure 13.8) and, in a very abstract manner, on the upper windows.

However, if the plans for Wright's temple or Corbusier's city are performing as "ornaments constructed," what are the ornaments ornamenting? In both examples, it could be argued, while the organizational geometries of the plans are not specifically ornamenting the subordinate elements of their buildings, they may be *ornamenting the landscapes or streetscapes* in which their buildings are situated. That argument requires that an "ornament constructed" be perceived as producing a metamorphosis in a larger ground or field of ornamentation.

But modern buildings in cities are hardly ever perceived as metamorphoses emerging out of or merging into their streetscapes. Even if the gridded streetscape were considered a geometric object ornamented by a building, it could not be considered a visual metamorphosis because it is visible only from the sky.

The early modernist efforts to pervade the body and plans of independent buildings with the geometric stuff of ornament actually fueled the idea that a building itself could be an *autonomous* work of art of the sort we are accustomed to viewing at galleries. The ornamental shaping of an entire building invites the whole building, by itself, to express the rhythmic drives of the chora or images of nature. The building in whole cloth could become a dramatic expression of Eros, like a shapely work of freestanding sculpture. By comparison, the traditionally ornamented work of architecture is constituted to express a limited amount of Eros, worldliness, and fantasy in combination with utility at a variety of scales. This multileveled system of visual language conserves the basic building's utilitarian identity as well as its essential tranquility, physics, and firmness.

The basic building, attempting in Kerr's sense to perform as ornament constructed, dominated Western architecture during the 1950s and 1960s. At first, buildings dissolved into patterns of geometric reg-

13.9 At first, buildings exhibited regular geometry. Project for an ideal city (Highrise City) by Ludwig Karl Hilbersheimer, 1924.

213

ularity (figure 13.9). Eventually, the regularized and homogeneous compositions attempted to overcome their own weight and location by rising into the air atop slender columns (figure 13.10). The same impulse toward weightlessness moved the articulation of building surfaces in the directions of transparency and reflectivity (figure 13.11).

When Eero Saarinen designed the United States Embassy Chancellery in London in 1955 (built 1956–60), he commented on his expressive strategy and his singularity of intent. "The character of expression of any building can only be achieved if it is itself a total expression. Like any work of art, it must be dominated by a strong, simple concept. All of its parts must be an active part of one dominant attitude."[89] In a separate statement, he added that "this concept has to be exaggerated and overstated and repeated in every part of its interior, so that wherever you are, inside or outside, the building sings with the same message."[90] In discussing the specific design of the embassy, which was located in a planned Georgian square, Saarinen stated that his manner of being sympathetic to the Georgian neighborhood was to consider "a continuity of material: the Portland stone which as trim and ornament on the red-brick pseudo-Georgian buildings becomes the material for the embassy."[91] The architect's admission that the building was composed into a relentless mononarrative and uniform materiality is slightly compromised by his inclusion of a rather autonomous bronze eagle on the roof over the entrance, relieved slightly by a jagged parapet along the horizon (figure 13.12).

In 1962, Paul Rudolph designed the new Art and Architecture building for Yale University as a composition of individually articulated building blocks connected tangentially in space like the intersecting elements in a Chinese puzzle rather than as visceral units of stone upon stone (figure 13.13). Although the tangential blocks congeal into a unified building, they provide very little information about the physics of construction in contrast to the rusticated stone elements constituting the vaults and lintels of traditional construction (figure 13.14). Thus on the most primary level of architectural language, in which the building seeks to explain its physical nature, the architecture of the Art and Architecture building focuses upon the abstract sculptural concept of "blockiness," even to the extent of identifying the windows as the openings of the leftover voids between the blocks. The surfaces of the blocks are further broken into sharp and jagged ribbons of lacerating concrete that aggravate the sense of touch. The movement toward an expression of brutality seems to explain the design as a singularly aggressive substitute for the more orchestrated distribution of playful-

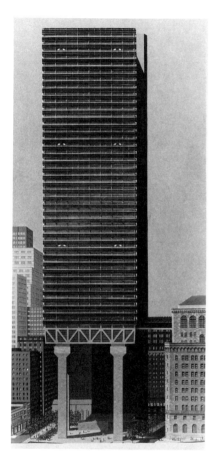

13.10 Rising into the air atop slender columns, buildings attempted to overcome their own weight. Roche and Dinkeloo, Federal Reserve Bank project, unbuilt, New York, 1969.

13.11 The impulse toward weightlessness seemed to inspire transparent and reflective building surfaces. Roche and Dinkeloo, United Nations Plaza Hotel, New York.

13.12 The uniformity of Saarinen's United States Embassy Chancellery in London is slightly relieved by a jagged parapet along the horizon of the roof.

13.13 Paul Rudolph's Art and Architecture building is composed of individual blocks connected like elements of a Chinese puzzle. Yale University, New Haven.

ly defensive, aggressive, and lyrical ornaments, such as foliation, gargoyles, and spearheads, that once secured entries and roofs. Unlike the protective griffins sparingly deposited on the eaves of Greek and Gothic building, the jagged and forbidding lacerations of the art and architecture building occupy virtually all of the building's surfaces, inside and out, as Saarinen insisted. Despite the elegance and excitement of the building, the act of incessantly delivering so much abrasive texture into the actual wall surfaces of the entire building forces the language of its architecture into a monofigural, rather than a polyfigural, form of expression.

Perhaps the culmination of the movement to produce monofigural artworks exhibiting sculptural contortion was in the writhing architecture of the late 1980s and early 1990s (figure 13.15). Such works can be marvelously aggressive by performing as action paintings, with walls and roofs of brush strokes. The attention-getting power of those works aside, it is revealing to compare their defiance of gravity and upright form to some examples of eighteenth-century rococo architecture, such as the interior of the pilgrimage church Die Wies in Bavaria (fig-

13.14 The visual articulation of vault and lintels provides clues about the physics of construction. Louis Sullivan, Carrie Eliza Getty Tomb, Graceland Cemetery, Chicago.

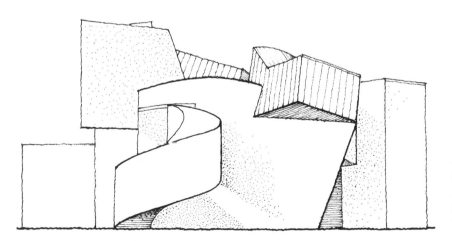

13.15 The writhing architecture of the late eighties was the culmination of the movement toward structural contortion. Drawing of Frank Gehry's Vitra Design Museum.

13.16 Gehry's attempt to defy gravity recalls a similar impulse manifest in 18th-century rococo architecture like that of Die Wies Pilgrimage Church, Bavaria.

ure 13.16). The rocaille ornament is distributed into the walls and transitional space in the upper reaches of the principal interior spaces and manages to disrupt the conventional elements below with a contrariness comparable to the skewed sections of a contorted building. Yet the proportions and disposition of the primary elements, such as the supporting columns, the upright perimeter walls, and the principal passages, remain quiet, edificial, and substantial (figure 13.17). In other words, despite its florid nature, the rococo architecture neither obfus-

13.17 While rococo ornament managed to disrupt conventions of construction, the interior columns, on the ground level, remained ordinary and substantial.

cates the primary expression of a conventional edifice nor fiercely contests the customary institutional, urban, or domestic types of building in order to proclaim, in *whole cloth*, a single message of turbulence. The figural moves in Die Weis are polyfigural and emergent into the life of the culture rather than monofigural and self-centered.

5. Ornament is too expensive. In a modern industrialized society, the normal costs of construction are reflected in standardized components. The expense of incorporatinging ornament is excessive.

In domestic architecture, the variations in the square-foot costs of modern construction are roughly in the four-hundred-percent range. The percentage of the building cost assigned to ornament per se could stretch from a fraction of one percent to one-third of the entire budget, although today it is more likely to be in the couple of percentage points. It is not difficult to calculate that the expense of ornament is readily available within the portion of building costs normally directed toward the refinement of architectural expression. Nevertheless, ornament is often excluded entirely, even in the greatest of budgets, on the grounds that it exceeds the requirements of architecture. This is obviously the stuff of rhetoric and prejudice rather than economics, especially considering that the production of ornament benefits also from modern technology and can be commensurately less expensive than it would have been in a traditional handcraft society. Note, too, that cost has never been a deterrent to the presence of ornament in the history of great architecture. Indeed, traditional cultures have produced remarkable ornament for thousands of years within both the least and the most expensive buildings and at all levels of society. In a lecture entitled "The Arts, High and Plain," the art historian George Kubler described a phenomenon in which the members of a culture previously dominated by a ruling aristocracy or a theocracy usually acquired the noble expressions of ornament for themselves after the demise of the ruling institution and before the ascent of another ruling institution.[92] Kubler described such interregnums between dominating authorities as "interludes of release." In the "interludes," the appropriated ornaments appeared upon everyday tools and clothing or on the conspicuous elements of small dwellings, where, for being sacred, they would have been prohibited as social imposture under the old regime. That is not a budget matter. When asked to cite a recent example of that kind of popular appropriation in Western culture, Kubler suggested that the emerging Victorian middle class, with its upholstered small parlors, polychrome wallpaper, and claw-footed chairs, was inspired by the articles of a declining aristocracy. If the Victorians were delighted by their new property, we must question subsequent criticisms of their bad taste and excess—or acknowledge those criticisms and still valorize the appropriation.

In regard to the charge of excess, it is important to emphasize the key economic feature of ornament, which is its alliance with utilitarian form. Because ornament engages the economic and the ordinary elements of construction, the typical ornamented building can, at its most primary

13.18, 13.19 A powerfully ornamented building can be a very straightforward structure. The Museum of Art by Ellis Lawrence at the University of Oregon, 1932.

level, be a rather straightforward structure (figures 13.18 and 13.19). If a measure of the extraordinary is expected from an ordinary work of architecture, and it often is, the issue of excess should be addressed only in comparison with the costs of alternate means of architectural expression. For example, what are the comparative costs of elaborating or composing the entire building to become a work of art in the sense of "ornament constructed," or employing materials of high expressive quality throughout the entire building, or installing paintings, sculptures, and other symbolic furnishings? Consider that technologically demonstrative construction is often quite expensive to build and maintain.

The concern regarding excessive cost is a fossil left over from moments when lavish ornament was an expression of wealth amidst poverty, a prejudice surviving from rhetoric more suited to the beginning of the twentieth century than to the beginning of the twenty-first.

6. Ornament is a dead language. It was a living language at an earlier stage of Western culture, when people both required and understood its special nature. Today we have other sufficient means of visual communication.

If the first part of this proclamation were true, we would not be able to read or understand ornament from the past in a natural or at least nonacademic way. How then can we explain the power or spell that great tracery or Islamic polychrome pattern still holds over those willing to see it? If we can experience the expansive energy of tracery, the microcosmic intricacy of Islamic pattern, and the rhythm of the ancient foliated scroll, the figures of ornament must be visually alive. Of course, this condition must be addressed on an individual basis by visiting the sites of ornament. Indeed, if we sense that ornament from the past is alive, how can we deposit its efficacy in the past or, put another way, how can we propose that the past is sequestered from the present rather than being a living part of the present?

The notion that a vivid art form from the past is dead might require that we wrap shrouds over the other art forms as well, and thus the Gregorian chant, traditional Indian dancing, Shakespeare, and Brahms could be buried once and for all. But many are still engaged by such great music, performance, and literature.

Could the proposed obituary for architectural ornament be based on the fact that ornament is a profoundly dependent rather than a radically free form of expression and thus not a truly modern art form? We must grant that the compositions of Shakespeare and Brahms belong to more "self-sufficient" art forms, at least to the extent that they are not dependent on coincident expressions of utility. But does ornament's implication with its objects of ornamentation make it any less a living form of expression? Does this suggest that an art form today must be independent and divorced from utility, or that it must be free from place to be a living language?

7. The narrative and imaginative content traditionally provided by ornament may be provided today by more independent art forms and need not be an essential property of architecture or a derivative of utility. The modern practice of situating art in architecture can be regarded as a substitute for ornament.

There are many eloquent examples of modern art-in-architecture, although there is nothing particularly modern about situating independent works of art in architectural space, as evidenced by the great equestrian statuary of antiquity or the Renaissance masterpieces placed on the walls of Italian palazzos. Indeed, both the objects we have come to call fine art and figures of ornament have forever coexisted in the space of great Western architecture. However, the notion that art-in-architecture is a substitute for ornament is faulty if the art under consideration is compositionally autonomous or self-sufficient. Autonomy is antithetical to the condition of dependence that is essential to ornament.

The imaginative escapades nourished by the fine arts of drawing, painting, and sculpture in recent times have acquired much of their prestige, pretenses of freedom, and the aura of "creativity" precisely by distancing themselves from the mundane articles of practicality. By the early twenty-first century, works of art have become increasingly portable.

By contrast, early modernist architecture moved to limit its medium of expression, that is, its fundamental kit of parts, to physical elements and spatial formations derived from the economics of construction and use. As a consequence, the visual disciplines of art, wrought from the unshackled world of the imagination, and an architecture developed from utility, have become locked into separate realms of thought and practice. To the extent that these professional distinctions reflect a fundamental cultural attitude, barriers appear to have been established between different potentials of our mental lives. We have not prohibited ourselves from moving from one potential to another, but rather we have allowed the distinct contents to become professionally and functionally divorced. This modern way of thinking seems to promote the authority vested in the clarity of hyperspecialization. In so specialized a view, expressions of work exist in moments other than play, and expressions of reality are discouraged from directly engaging with fantasy.

The discipline and media of ornament act *against* the clarity of hyper-specialization, which is subtly condoned in most modern practices of pure art as compared to pure architecture. Ornament's metamorphoses are heterogeneous as they manifest multiple ways of thinking and thematize the heterogeneity of our internal and external life worlds. In the art of building, they combine the actual with the imaginary and memorable features of the places in which we dwell, have dwelled, and wish to dwell. Ornament, with its extended vocabulary, articulates the psychological fact that we can imagine in many cultural, social, and psychological places at once. It also resists the notions of completeness suggested by "pure" works of art in works of architecture, in which the medium and expressive vocabulary of one or the other discipline are limited to a short list of typical professional parts.

8. Ornament has been traditionally associated with religions and ethnic groups as well as with institutions of power and wealth. Because it has emblematized such authoritative and self-interested groups, ornament is not appropriate in the public realms of a modern democratic and multicultural state.

This cautious political approach is quite common in both the classroom and public councils. Somehow ornament has become overassociated with its previous clients, be they dictators, aristocrats, religious or ethnic constituencies. In chapter 10, "Appropriation, Reappropriation, and Relocation," I reviewed this concern, including

Quatremère de Quincy's fear that overreacting to prior associations could have a catastrophic effect on the arts.

It is inappropriate to borrow specific ornaments from any living institution, particularly a vulnerable institution, that holds its seminal or particularized ornaments to be sacred in the present. Contemporary American Indians fall somewhat into this category, along with some vital minority religions such as Judaism. However, the great systems of ornament from the seminal Western cultures of the ancient Greeks and medieval Europeans do not belong in this category. My lengthy review of the foliated scroll, in chapter 6, reveals an ancient Greek formulation that has diffused through many cultures. It has traveled the world and become its public property. Gothic tracery has moved from the ecclesiastical to the domestic and the collegiate over hundreds of years and over many political and ethnic boundaries. In both the foliated scroll and in tracery we are witnessing something more profound than the display of intellectual or cultural property belonging only to a certain constituency. We are looking at the fundamental organizational shaping of visual thought belonging to a basic level of expression. Indeed, the great perduring systems of ornament must be understood as belonging to a domain of human thought capable of multiple interpretation and nearly infinite reworking.

Observe what has *actually* taken place in many public settings in the United States that are particularly devoid of ornament. Rather than

13.20 Public space has become visually privatized through the spectacle of corporate and commercial logos and signage.

13.21 The Chrysler building belonged to a corporation but provided a majestic public symbol in the form of a spire.

remaining politically uncommitted voids or becoming undifferentiated spaces in the egalitarian sense, public space has become visually privatized by virtue of a spectacle of corporate and commercial logos and signage (figure 13.20). The spectacle of private property and privatized power virtually controls the visual life in the unornamented spaces of the recently built public realm. Isn't it curious that in the earlier years of the twentieth century, when ornament was more profusive and capitalism was rampant, the visible emblems of private ownership were more recessive? In the late nineteenth century and the early years of the twentieth century, American cities were a riot of both eclectic and experimental ornament. The Chrysler Building, for example, belonged to a corporation, but it gave New York City a majestic spire

225

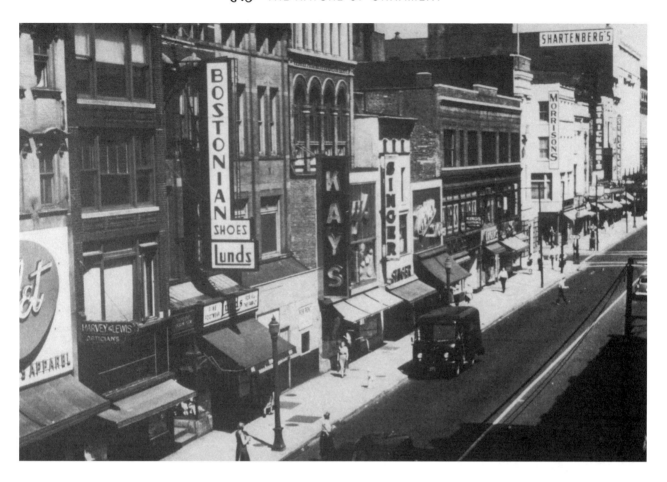

13.22 On Main Street, Byzantine and classical facades, Deco store-fronts, and Victorian parapets stood side by side in an orderly manner. New Haven.

(figure 13.21). On Main Street, the ornament of Byzantine and classical facades stood side by side with Victorian parapets and deco store-fronts (figure 13.22). Animals, foliations, and all manner of metamorphoses lurked in the niches and along the friezes (figure 13.23). Visual signs announcing the owners of those buildings were more discreet, often appearing on small bronze plaques in large buildings or in terracotta inscriptions along the entablatures of small commercial buildings (figure 13.24). A sense of publicness was dominant. During the same period, our college campuses exhibited a collection of Victorian curiosities, collegiate tracery, Romanesque demons, and ivy-covered Georgian capitals.

Critics of those eclectic and marvelously embellished downtowns and campuses were known to deplore what they described as romantic pastiche. They called for a more pure, regular, unifying style. But consider the consequences of a sanitized style of architecture stripped of its layers of conventional historical reference, including the conven-

13.23 Animals lurked in the niches and along the friezes. Unidentified, France, 13th century.

13.24 The signs of ownership are discreetly displayed with a small bronze plaque upon Sullivan's Carson Pirie Scott Department Store, in Chicago.

tionalized distributions of ornament. How, in the context of such a uniformity, do we find our way? What architectural clues are there, in the unspecified and regularized geometry of windows, doorways, and passageways, or in the blankness of the plaza, that point us toward a particular residence, office, or meeting place? How do we escape a feeling of being displaced or being nowhere in particular?

Written signs and numbers indicating specific streets or addresses have become more and more necessary to enable us to get from point to point. Our destinations are prescribed on charts, on

13.25 *A profusion of distracting numbers, letters, and even banners have become substitutes for feeling our way architecturally. Corner of Chapel and Temple Streets on the historic New Haven Green.*

13.26 Vehicular entrance to the Bronx Zoo, New York. Paul Manship, 1925.

maps, or with verbal directions (figure 13.25). In the absence of more familiar and more traditionally embellished buildings, gates (figure 13.26), and urban furnishings, a profusion of numbers, letters, and documented information has become a substitute for seeing or feeling our way architecturally. In other words, the regularized "democratic" void is an ideological promise that—beyond its vacuity—in reality cannot function in the thick of most modern cities unless it is pasted over with writing and numerical information systems of the kind we also employ in way-finding on bookshelves, in storage facilities, or with the diagrams often found in instruction manuals.

14.1 Tapestries of patterned sawdust momentarily establish a transcendent place and a sense of repose in the downtown of Huamantla, Mexico.

PLACE AND REPOSE

Human beings fashion an environment
for themselves, a space to live in, suggested
by their patterns of life and constructed
around whatever symbols of reality seem
important to them.

Vincent Scully[93]

By once again becoming a more expansive medium and system of communication, architecture would more generously represent our world. The limited kit of parts, rooted in the weary century-old promise of a simple, more efficient, and heroic technology, is too specialized. In fact, the global industrialization of building technology has produced an architectural monotony that belies the world's various cultures, landscapes, and species. But even such a homogenous basic vocabulary could fuel the fulfillment of architectural expression if it were to admit ornament, at scales from the domestic to the urban. Ornament could fulfill the world picture—as it often did in earlier centuries, when building technologies had also no doubt become monotonous over time. By incorporating visions of the world at large and convening with ordinary and profane things, ornament can articulate the complexity and mythology of particular times and places.

"Place is an event," writes the philosopher Edward Casey, "a matter of taking place. . . . It is the event of envelopment itself."[94] In this respect, the act of ornamenting can be as much the cultural proclaiming of place as the informing of a utilitarian object. Ornament gives luster to its objects and to the event of envelopment. This positive act is also defensive, in that it shields the object or place from the dreadful anonymity of an existence out of place, from being simply a denoted thing or only a utility or merely a parcel of land. Ornament exalts ordinary properties by incorporating extraordinary images and individuals' memories within patterns that can simultaneously intermingle with a particular history and with local flora and fauna. Like the Turtle Dance of the Taos Indians, ornament can register place as a living event.

Yet, in the authoritative words of Owen Jones, ornament "should possess fitness, proportions, harmony, the result of which is *repose* . . . that repose which the mind feels when the eye, the intellect, and affections are satisfied."[95] How then do we reconcile this apparent expectation of tranquility and restfulness with ornament's visual dynamism, stridently exclaimed by the struggling nature of its foot and line work? How can the presence of configurations that are often the most turbulent, such as the visual activity we find in Gothic tracery, the rococo cartouche, and Sullivan's efflorescent ornament, contribute to the harmony of repose? Perhaps John Ruskin's notion of "active rigidity" and Sullivan's phrase "dynamic equilibrium" (see chapter 4) help portray the necessary combination of movement and rest. One function of ornament has always been to marshall extremes, to hold many things and to bring many distinct actions into one limited composition. Ornament struggles to serve its ancient purpose, which is to bring order and produce cosmos out of chaos. The cosmos per se may be tranquil, but it harbors discord and tendencies toward fragmentation as the Eros within it seeks to control strife and conflict. Great ornament neither negates strife nor moves to anesthetize or homogenize passion with a colorless veil of morbid geometry. To the contrary, it resides and revels in the convergence of differences, dislocations, and conflicts.

To repose, and to *ornament*, is therefore to momentarily register a reposition, that is, a redisposition of scattered bits of ourselves, our earth, and our sky in an intense, rhythmic, and restful state—and to do so in the fabric of our useful, everyday objects.

NOTES

1. Henri Focillon, *The Life of Forms in Art* (New York: Zone Books, 1992), p. 18. (Originally published as *La vie des formes* in 1934.)
2. John Summerson, *Heavenly Mansions* (New York: W. W. Norton, 1963), p. 215.
3. Indra Kragis McEwen, *Socrates' Ancestor* (Cambridge, MA: MIT Press, 1993), p. 44.
4. George Hersey, *The Lost Meaning of Classical Architecture* (Cambridge, MA: MIT Press, 1988), p. 149.
5. Vitruvius, *The Ten Books on Architecture*, trans. Morris Hicky Morgan (New York: Dover Publications, 1960), p. 104.
6. Otto Jon Simpson, *The Gothic Cathedral* (Princeton: Princeton University Press, 1956), p. 29.
7. Ibid., p. 420.
8. Ibid., p. 183.
9. Karsten Harries, *The Bavarian Rococo Church* (New Haven: Yale University Press, 1983), p. 192.
10. Ibid., p. 195.
11. Christopher Dresser, *The Art of Decorative Design* (Watkins Glen, NY: American Life Foundation, 1977), p. 1. (Originally published by Day and Son: London, 1862.)
12. The *Encyclopædia Britannica*, eleventh edition, vol. xx (New York: Encyclopædia Britannica, Inc., 1911), p. 298.
13. Ibid.
14. George Kubler, *The Shape of Time: Remarks on the History of Things* (New Haven: Yale University Press, 1962), p. vii.
15. Mary H. Helms, "Cosmovision of the Chiefdoms of the Isthmus of Panama," in *The Ancient Americas*, ed. Richard Townsend (Munich: Art Institute of Chicago, 1992), p. 227.
16. John Ruskin, *The Seven Lamps of Architecture* (New York: Noonday Press, 1977), p. 41 (Originally published in 1849.)
17. Mary LeCron Foster, paper delivered at the conference *Giving the Body Its Due* (University of Oregon, Eugene, OR, November 4, 1989).
18. Samuel Taylor Coleridge, "Poesy and Art," in *Aesthetic Theories: Studies in the Philosophy of Art*, eds. Karl Aschenbrenner and Arnold Isenberg (Englewood Cliffs, NJ: Prentice-Hall, 1965), p. 266.
19. Francoise Henry, *The Book of Kells* (New York: Alfred A. Knopf, 1974), p. 205.
20. The linguistic function of rhythm is discussed in more detail in chapter 6 and demonstrated in chapter 7.
21. Focillon, p. 67.
22. A. D. F. Hamlin, *A History of Ornament* (New York: The Century Co., 1928), p. 6.
23. Edward N. Kaufman, "Architectural Representation in Victorian England," *Journal of the Society of Art Historians* 46:30-38 (March 1987), p. 37.
24. Ibid., p. 35.
25. John Ruskin, "The Nature of Gothic," in *The Stones of Venice*, ed. Jan Morris (Boston: Little, Brown & Co., 1981), p. 121. (Originally published in [1851–3].)
26. Louis H. Sullivan, "Emotional Architecture as Compared with Intellectual: a Study in Subjective and Objective," in *Kindergarten Chats and Other Writings* (New York: Dover Publications, 1979), p. 200. (Originally published in *Lippincott's*, March 1896.)
27. John Ruskin, *The Seven Lamps of Architecture* (New York: The Noonday Press, 1977), p. 110. (Originally published in 1849.)
28. Louis H. Sullivan, *A System of Architectural Ornament According with a Philosophy of Man's Powers* (The Eakin's Press, 1963), p. 4. (Originally published in 1922.)
29. Theodore Turak, "French and English Sources of Sullivan's Ornament and Doctrines," *The Prairie School Review* 11:4 (fourth quarter, 1974), pp. 5–29.
30. Roland Barthes, *The Responsibility of Forms*, trans. Richard Howard (New York: Hill and Wang, 1985), p. 248.
31. Jerome Pollitt, *The Ancient View of Greek Art* (New Haven: Yale University Press, 1974), p. 138.
32. Ibid.
33. Ibid., p. 139.
34. Ibid., p. 23.
35. Julia Kristeva, *The Kristeva Reader*, ed. Toril Moi (New York: Columbia University Press, 1986), p. 93.
36. Ibid., pp. 95–96.
37. Amittai F. Aviram, *Telling Rhythm* (Ann Arbor: University of Michigan Press, 1994), p. 177.
38. Ibid., p. 229.
39. Ibid.
40. Ernst Gombrich, *The Sense of Order* (Ithaca: Cornell University Press, 1979), p. 171.
41. Louis H. Sullivan, "The Tall Office Building Artistically Considered," in *Kindergarten Chats and Other Writings* (New

York: Dover, 1979), p. 208. (Originally published in *Lippincott's*, March 1896.)

42. Ibid., p. 203.

43. William Jordy, *Louis Sullivan: The Function of Ornament,* ed. Wim de Wit, (New York: W. W. Norton, 1986), p. 76.

44. Focillon, p. 67.

45. Adam Phillips, *Winnicott* (Cambridge, MA: Harvard University Press, 1988), p. 5.

46. Ibid., p. 7.

47. Ibid., p. 5.

48. Focillon, pp. 65–66.

49. Ibid., p. 113.

50. Erwin Panofsky, *Gothic Architecture and Scholasticism* (Ontario, Canada: New American Library, 1957), p. 45.

51. Suzanne Langer quoting Arthur Michel in *Feeling and Form* (New York: Charles Scribner's Sons, 1953), pp. 185–86.

52. McEwen, p. 81.

53. Kent Bloomer and Charles Moore, *Body, Memory, and Architecture* (New Haven: Yale University Press, 1977), p. 41.

54. Ibid., p. 41.

55. John Summerson, "What Is Ornament and What Is Not," *VIA III* (The Graduate School of Fine Arts, University of Pennsylvania, 1977), p. 7.

56. Alexander Tzonis and Liane Lefaivre, *Classical Architecture: The Poetics of Order* (Cambridge, MA: MIT Press, 1986), p. 119.

57. Summerson, *Heavenly Mansions,* p. 9.

58. Joan Evans, *Pattern,* vol. 1 (Oxford: Clarendon Press, 1931), p. 6.

59. Ibid.

60. Sylvia Lavin, *Quatremère de Quincy and the Invention of a Modern Language of Architecture* (Cambridge, MA: MIT Press, 1992), pp. 164–65.

61. See *Winterthur Portfolio,* vol. 27 (Chicago: University of Chicago Press, 1992), pp. 145–70.

62. Ibid., p. 163.

63. J. B. Jackson, *The Necessity for Ruins* (Amherst: University of Massachusetts Press, 1980), pp. 78–79.

64. Michel Foucault, "Of Other Spaces," *Architecture—Mouvement—Continuité* (October 1984); translated by Jay Miskowiec; republished in *Diacritics* (Spring 1986), p. 22.

65. Ibid., p. 23.

66. Ibid.

67. John Ruskin, *The Seven Lamps of Architecture,* p. 137.

68. Nicholas Adams with Janet Reno, RES 22, *Journal of Archeology and Aesthetics* (Cambridge, MA: Peabody Museum of Archaeology and Ethnology, Harvard University, 1992), p. 165.

69. Amelia Peck, ed., *Alexander Jackson Davis* (New York: Rizzoli, 1992), pp. 54–55.

70. Esther McCoy, "Mosaics—Juan O'Gorman," *Arts and Architecture* (February 1959), p. 12.

71. Juan O'Gorman, "Arquitecto y Pintor," Universidad Nacional Autónoma de México, Primera Edición (1982), p. 121.

72. Ibid.

73. Ibid., p. 122.

74. Esther McCoy, p. 12.

75. Octavio Paz, review of Mexican Churches by Eliot Porter and Ellen Auerbach, *The New York Times Book Review* (December 20, 1987.), p. 25.

76. Erik Scott McCready, *Nebraska History* (Lincoln: Nebraska Historical Society, Fall 1974), p. 362.

77. Ibid., p. 381.

78. Orville H. Zabel, *Nebraska History* (Lincoln: Nebraska State Historical Society, Fall 1981), p. 294.

79. Richard Oliver, *Bertram Grosvenor Goodhue* (Cambridge, MA: MIT Press, 1983), p. 226.

80. Le Corbusier, *Towards a New Architecture,* trans. Frederick Etchells (London: The Architectural Press, 1927), p. 19.

81. Colin St. John Wilson, *Architectural Reflections* (Oxford, England: Butterworth Architecture, 1992), p. 207.

82. Ellery S. Husted, "The Sterling Memorial Library," *The Yale University Library Gazette* 5:4 (April 1931), p. 57.

83. Ibid., p. 81.

84. Hugh Morrison, *Louis Sullivan* (New York: W. W. Norton, 1935), p. 201.

85. Henry-Russell Hitchcock and Philip Johnson, *The International Style* (New York: W. W. Norton, 1966), p. 69. (Originally published in 1922.)

86. James Trilling, "The Flight from Enchantment," in *The Yale Review,* ed. J. D. McClatchy (Boston: Blackwell Publishers, April 1998), p. 86.

87. Ibid., p. 98.

88. Karsten Harries, *The Ethical Function of Architecture* (Cambridge, MA: MIT Press, 1997), p. 48.

89. Aline B. Saarinen, ed., *Eero Saarinen on His Work* (New Haven: Yale University Press, 1968), p. 10.

90. Ibid.

91. Ibid., p. 56.

92. George Kubler, "Art High and Plain," lecture delivered at the Yale School of Architecture, October 31, 1975.

93. Vincent Scully, *Architecture: The Natural and the Manmade.* (New York: St. Martin's Press, 1991), p. 1.

94. Edward S. Casey, *The Fate of Place.* (Berkeley: University of California Press, 1997), p. 295.

95. Owen Jones, *The Grammar of Ornament* (London: Studio Editions, 1986), proposition 4, p. 5. (originally published in 1856.)

CREDITS

Figure 1.1: From Victore Marie Charles Ruprich-Robert, *Flore Ornementale* (Paris: Dunod, 1876).

Figure 1.2: From Claude Bragdon, *The Frozen Fountain* (New York: Alfred A. Knopf, 1932).

Figure 1.3: From *Encyclopedia Brittanica,* 1943 edition.

Figure 1.6: From A. D. F. Handlin, *A History of Ornament* (New York: Century Co., 1916).

Figure 1.10: From Joseph Gauthier and Louis Capelle, *Traite de Composition* (Paris: Librairie Plon, 1911).

Figure 2.6: James Mejuto, courtesy of Lyndhurst, a National Trust Historic Site.

Figure 3.3: From *The Book of Kells* (London: Thames and Hudson, 1974).

Figures 3.5 and 3.6: From Joseph Gauthier and Louis Capelle, *Traite de Composition.*

Figure 3.7: Painting by Jean de Blondel. From Michel Melot, *The Art of Illustration* (New York: Rizzoli, 1984).

Figure 3.8: ©Cervin Robinson.

Figure 3.9: Courtesy of Brent C. Brolin.

Figure 3.10: From Janet S. Byrne, *Renaissance Prints and Drawings* (New York: The Metropolitan Museum of Art, 1981).

Figure 3.11: From *The Book of Kells.*

Figure 3.12: Courtesy of Brent C. Brolin.

Figure 3.13: From George Hersey, *The Lost Meaning of Classical Architecture.* Beinecke Rare Book and Manuscript Library, Yale University.

Figure 4.1: From Andrea Palladio, *Quattro Libri di Architettura* (London, 1715). Beinecke Rare Book and Manuscript Library, Yale University.

Figure 4.3: From Diana S. Waite, *Architectural Elements* (Princeton, NJ: Pyne Press; N.D.).

Figure 4.6: From Sir Thomas Graham Jackson, *Architecture* (London: MacMillan, 1925).

Figure 4.10: ©Cervin Robinson.

Figure 4.11: Courtesy Thomas Beeby.

Figure 4.12: From Victore Marie Charles Ruprich-Robert, *Flore Ornementale.*

Figure 4.17: Courtesy George Thomas.

Figure 6.1: From Francois Dumas, *The Temple of Dendura* (Cairo: Ministère de la Culturel Centre de Documentation et D'Etude sur l'Anciene Egypte, 1970).

Figure 6.47: Amelianburg, Spiegelsaal. From *The Bavarian Rococo Church* by Karsten Harries. Yale University Press, New Haven (1983). Bayerische Verwaltung der staatlichen Schlosser, Garten und Seen.

Figure 6.48: From *Baroque and Rococo: Architecture and Decoration,* ed. Anthony Blunt (New York: Portland House, 1988).

Figure 6.52: From Christopher Dresser, *Modern Ornamentation* (London: B. T. Batsford, 1886).

Figure 6.53: ©Cervin Robinson.

Figure 7.1: Courtesy of Brent C. Brolin.

Figure 7.2: Illustration by Jason Gaddis, after Jessica Rawson, *Chinese Ornament* (London: Published for the Trustees of the British Museum by British Museum Publications Ltd., 1984).

Figure 7.3: From Alexander Speltz, *Styles of Ornament* (1904–1906; reprint, New York: Grosset & Dunlap, 1935).

Figure 7.5: ©Cervin Robinson.

Figure 7.12: From Owen Jones, *The Grammar of Ornament* (London: Day and Son, 1856).

Figure 8.1: From *Encyclopedia Brittanica,* 1943 edition.

Figure 8.8: From *Encyclopedia Brittanica,* 1943 edition.

Figures 8.9 and 8.10, 8.12–8.22: Illustrations by Rebecca Smith and Kent Bloomer.

Figure 9.1: Courtesy Pueblo Cultural Center, Albuquerque, NM.

Figure 9.8: From Andrea Palladio, *Quattro Libri di Architettura.* Beinecke Rare Book and Manuscript Library, Yale University.

Figure 9.9: From Daniel Barbaro, *I Dieci Libri dell'architettura di M. Vitruvio* (Venice, 1570). Beinecke Rare Book and Manuscript Library, Yale University.

Figure 9.10: From Alexander Tzonis and Liane Lefaivre, *Classical Architecture: The Poetics of Order* (Cambridge, MA: MIT Press, 1986).

Figure 9.17: Illustration by William Hersey.

Figure 9.21: Illustration by Sophie Hampshire.

Figures 10.1–10.4: Courtesy of the Library of Congress, Geography and Map Division.

Figure 10.5: Warder Collection.

Figure 10.6: National Graphic Center.

Figures 10.7 and 10.8: Architect of the Capitol Collection, Prints and Photographs Division, Library of Congress.

Figure 10.9: Courtesy of the Connecticut Historical Society.

Figure 10.10: Wayne Andrews©ESTO. All rights reserved.

Figure 11.1: Illustration by Jason Gaddis, after Eve Blau, *Ruskinian Gothic* (Princeton, NJ: Princeton University Press, 1982).

Figure 11.3: Sarah Fox-Pitt, London, England.

Figure 11.9: All rights reserved, Metropolitan Museum of Art. Harris Brisbane Dick Fund, 1924. [24.66.419].

INDEX